In loving memory of my father,

Floyd Phillip Foss

1921~2011

Five Understandable Words

presents

Freedom's Foundation

SF Foss

FOXWARE PUBLISHING LLC

Las Cruces, New Mexico

For information go to: www.fiveunderstandablewords.com

Five Understandable Words and its logo are registered with the USPTO, Alexandria, VA, 22314.

Unless otherwise noted, all Biblical references are taken from the *New American Standard* Bible, ©1960, 1962, 1963, 1968, 1971, 1972, 1973, 1975, 1977, 1995 by the Lockman Foundation. Used by permission. (www.Lockman.org)

ISBN: 978-0-9964082-0-2

Printed in the USA

Cover photography: Tony McMehan
Cover design: John Griffin

Freedom's Foundation, Large Print Edition, is available at: www.amazon.com or www.foxwarepublishing.com or www.5understandablewords.com.

UNDERSTANDABLE 5 WORDS

Preface

Two thousand years ago, under the inspiration of God's Holy Spirit, the apostle Paul wrote to the church in Corinth that he preferred five understandable words be spoken when instructing than for ten thousand words to be used that cannot be understood. [1 Cor. 14:18] When I wrestled with this phrase, I asked God to reveal the significance of its meaning. This brought a new perspective to my Bible study and the result of which in-part is revealed through this book.

In these pages I have sought to present a biblical progression for the precepts of freedom through the medium of short five word phrases from the Bible. I do not claim to present an exhaustive rendering of such, only to reveal those obvious foundational values of which the Founders were intimately familiar, using the rich resource of the Bible's perspective in law and history to develop America's founding documents.

In President Abraham Lincoln's proclamation appointing a national day for fasting and prayer, he stated:

"It is the duty of nations... to recognize the sublime truth announced in the Holy Scriptures and proven by all history that those nations only are blessed whose God is the Lord... but we have forgotten God. We have forgotten the gracious hand which preserved us in peace and multiplied and enriched and strengthened us, and we have vainly imagined in the deceitfulness of our hearts that all these blessings were produced by some superior wisdom and virtue of our own. Intoxicated with unbroken success, we have become too self-sufficient to feel the necessity of redeeming and preserving grace – too proud to pray to the God that made us."

Source: Lincoln, Abraham; <u>Complete Works of Abraham Lincoln</u>, John G. Nicolay and John Hay, Vol. VIII, pp. 235-236, "Proclamation Appointing a National Fast Day, March 30, 1863.

My hope is, as you are introduced to the five word scriptural phrases, you will be encouraged to devote time in prayer and fasting for a spiritual awakening across our land in our time. Please encourage pastors in your communities to lead their people in sacred supplications for America, using this resource to unite people in forty days of focused prayer to advance freedom around the world.

I wish to thank those who have helped in the development of this work:

To my wife, Sandra, our daughters, Nicole and Natalie, our extended families, and our friends for wonderful celebrations of freedom enjoyed through the years. From Memorial Day to Independence Day, the times we celebrated the host of family activities: cookouts, singing, swimming, games, and fireworks will always be cherished.

To my father who has always been my hero, and to all who have served our nation sacrificing family, time, life, and limb for the liberties we enjoy, you have given so much.

To my editors: my wife, Sandra; my aunt, Nancy Welborn; David Harrison, James Manship, and Jim Fox; for their attention to detail and desire to deliver an excellent product.

To David Barton and the Wallbuilders organization for the excellent organization and availability of their online resources that are being used to preserve and promote long forgotten historical archives. The Wallbuilders Pastor's Briefings are exceptional! Churches, please budget resources for your pastor(s) to attend at least one – it's well worth it!

To Don Foster, Jonathan Fry, and Dr. John Trent for their insight and counsel.

To my prayer partners: Tony McMehan, Mitch Lowder, Lanny Bernard, Capt. Brad McDonald (USN, Ret.), Maj. David Freeman (USAF, Ret.), Brian Cuff, and Brett Schomaker. All your prayers are most precious to this writer. Your lives have been such a rich blessing to me.

Thank you.

Foreword

There are two reasons why I'm honored to write the foreword for this book filled with stories of faith and freedom, authored by a pastor, patriot, and good friend, Steve Foss.

First, while the idea and goal of freedom was constantly on the lips and hearts of those who founded our country, it's a term we rarely talk about today - except in shaking our head as we read from our iPad or watch cable news, and say in our heart, or out loud, "There's another aspect of our freedom that has been lost!" This book will remind you that with God's love and word, the real freedom He offers isn't just something for yesterday, but for today.

The 40 reflections that follow will give you timeless insights and practical examples, word studies, and the very words spoken by many of those who founded our country - foundational truths about our faith and freedom.

That's the first reason to read this book. It will help you remember what was so powerful about freedom at the founding of our country, and encourage you to bring freedom and life to your heart and family as well.

There's a second reason to read this book.

While *Freedom's Foundation* is filled with hope, it is being published at a time when our freedoms are eroding around us. It's not unlike the world C.S. Lewis saw and wrote about in 1957. In one of his last books, titled, "Delinquents in the Snow," Lewis speaks out against what he saw eroding freedom in his day, saying...

"At present, the very uncomfortable position is this: the State protects us less because it is unwilling to protect us against criminals at home and manifestly grows less and less able to protect us against foreign enemies. At the same time it demands from us more and more. We seldom had fewer rights and liberties, nor more burdens and we get less security in return. While our obligations increase their moral ground is taken away."

Think how contemporary Lewis' words are in our day! We live in a time that is more lawless at home, and more dangerous abroad then perhaps ever before. And we have a government that seems to ignore the dangers around us, and instead embraces platforms and endorses practices that are moving us away from any kind of moral ground!

And there again is the reason you need to read this book. The daily encouragement you'll find in *Freedom's Foundation*, will give you the one thing that will never change or erode: God's word.

Here, you and I can find God's life-giving wisdom that can guide us toward liberty: His heart that can free us; His love that can change us; and His Spirit Who can strengthen us and give us courage.

So enjoy, as I did, these 40 "foundational" pictures of freedom. Each one is indeed a bedrock way of looking at freedom and a platform for building wisdom into our lives, even in these confusing, challenging times.

May "God's freedom ring" more clearly in your heart for having read this book...

John Trent, Ph.D.
Gary Chapman Chair of Marriage and Family,
Ministry and Therapy
Moody Theological Seminary
Chicago, Illinois

(Our inalienable rights)
"...are not to be rummaged for among old parchments
or musty records.
They are written,
as with a sunbeam,
in the whole volume
of human nature
by the hand of the Divinity itself and can
never be erased
or obscured by mortal power."

Alexander Hamilton

Source: The Works of Alexander Hamilton, John Church Hamilton, editor.

Table of Contents

UNDERSTANDABLE 5 WORDS

"The heavens declare

His righteousness..."

Psalm 97:6

In this Psalm, David seeks to expose the reader to the obvious evidence that God is real. He describes how creation points to a Creator: the clouds, fire, lightning, the mountains, and then the awesome wonder of the heavens. The idea of the heavens declaring God's attribute of righteousness may seem somewhat baffling.

What traits about the sun, moon, and stars reflect his righteousness? Perhaps it's in the meaning of the word 'righteousness' that we see a fuller understanding of just what the heavens are declaring. The Hebrew word for righteousness is, "צִדְקוֹ" (pronounced, ṣiḏ-qōw). It carries the meaning of '*accurate and fair*', thus implying integrity.

It seems that God is speaking through His Word to teach us that He has designed an eco-system in which we all have a *fair* chance at life. The Bible tells us that the sun shines and the rain falls on both the just and the unjust (Matthew 5:45). I can't think of a better example to illustrate God's fairness to us. Those who study the creation both on macro and micro levels see the *accuracy* with which all things are designed and are held together to function properly in the cause-effect cosmos in which we exist. Space reveals God's glory by its sheer size. Yet, the Bible tells us the entire universe can be measured in the span of God's hand. (Isaiah 40:12)

The accuracy of the orbits and metaphysical laws that keep galaxies and stars in check point to a great plan that reflects His glory found in His righteousness - the integrity of His *accuracy* and *fairness*.

So, what does this mean to the follower of Jesus Christ? How is this to be applied in our daily lives? God's righteousness is to be revealed in and through us as we seek *accuracy* and thoroughness in our work. The Christ follower is not to be slack in work, but to work as if it were for God Himself, (Ephesians 6:7; Colossians 3:23) only satisfied with excellence in the completed work, just as God saw His work and said it was good. (Genesis 1:31)

A free society is secured on production with integrity, guaranteed only by honest owners and managers, as well as a workforce that embraces the integrity of accountability.

We reflect God's *fairness* by our treatment of others. We are to have fair and accurate scales and practices. (Proverbs 11:11; Leviticus 19:36) If we take it to the next level, we will apply this same fairness in our dealings with our neighbors, in our laws, judicial system, and national policies.

The righteousness, then, declared from the heavens is God's statement of His mercies that are extended to each generation through the creation and the systems within it to provide each of us a fair chance at pursuing life, liberty, and happiness. It was there from the beginning of time. When God's Spirit hovered over the waters, (Genesis 1:2) there was the seed of liberty being released around the world, for "...where the spirit of the Lord is there is liberty." (2 Corinthians 3:17)

It is this freedom that is declared from the heavens! The righteousness of God sets us free and is an essential part of freedom's foundation.

"Proclaim liberty throughout all the land,
to all the inhabitants thereof ... "
Leviticus 25:10 (KJV)

(Note: The Liberty Bell was so named after this verse. The verse is emblazoned upon it. **Source:** 110th Congress, 1st Session, H. RES. 888)

As you make intercession for this nation, give thanksgiving for those founding leaders who acted upon the heavenly evidence of freedom for all.

"...for your light has come..."

Isaiah 60:1

"...for your light has come..."

In this passage, Isaiah makes the contrast between a society that embraces God's principles and those that reject God's way. It's a simple distinction of light piercing darkness. Like a lighthouse, a society that espouses truth and fairness will be a beacon the world will seek out. The prophet Isaiah said it this way, *"Nations will come to your light, and kings to the brightness of your dawn."* (Isaiah 60:3)

The Psalmist describes God's Word as *"a lamp for my feet and a light on my path"*; (Psalm 119:105) thus, the importance of knowing and walking in God's Word which provides the light essential for maintaining the Believer's perspective. God's plan from the beginning of His covenant with Abraham was to bless the entire world through the Light He would bring to the nations. (Genesis 22:18)

When you enter a dark room, what is the first thing you do? You turn on a light, right? Light keeps you from stumbling over or running into things, and enables you to accurately identify possessions and people. When Jesus came to earth He brought the light of heaven to earth. Heaven's Light (Read John 1) helps us to avoid the stumbling blocks of life.

King Solomon created a list of these stumbling blocks in Proverbs 6:16-19 when he listed seven things that are detestable in God's sight:

1. A proud look
2. A lying tongue
3. Hands that shed innocent blood
4. A heart that devises wicked plots
5. Feet that are swift to run into mischief
6. A deceitful witness that speaks lies
7. One that creates discord among others

Paul created a similar list for the Galatians. He described them as deeds done under the veil of darkness:

♦sexual immorality ♦impurity ♦debauchery ♦idolatry ♦witchcraft
♦hatred ♦discord ♦jealousy ♦fits of rage ♦selfish ambition ♦dissensions
♦factions ♦envy ♦drunkenness ♦orgies ♦and the like. (Galatians 5:19-21)

These are the obstacles for those without the light of God and must not be named among those who believe in Jesus as Savior. However, in this world we will have trouble, and when we stumble, the result can be serious, even catastrophic. Spiritually speaking, stumbling renders the spiritual sojourner ineffective for God's work until confession is made, leading to recovery and restoration. This is why time spent in God's Word is so essential.

Light is necessary to correctly identify:

♦ friends or foes ♦ delights or distresses
♦ the ordinary from the extraordinary

Light provides the environment for our God-given senses to focus and to distinguish the critical details. Heaven's Light allows us the same abilities in the spiritual realm. The Christ follower has discernment to:

♦ identify those with kindred hearts
♦ avoid actions that will bring sorrow
♦ see the hand of God in daily life, thus providing a perspective to benefit one's family, work, and community.

When we utilize the light of God's Word, we avoid the collisions that can devastate our personal and family life. Without Heaven's Light, one becomes part of the darkness. Jesus said it this way, *"If then the light within you is darkness, how great is that darkness!"* (Matthew 6:23) Without the Light of the world to direct our thoughts and actions, we end up with the blind leading the blind. We become part of the darkness. Truth is a necessary component of freedom's foundation for freedom to thrive in an environment nourished by integrity and fairness.

Finally, light is also a source of life. Plants turn toward the sun drinking in its energy. Plants have light-sensing proteins, catalysts that turn a plant toward the light. As they grow, systems develop to reproduce or replicate. This design is in all life, both plant and animal – a program to reproduce.

The Light of the world (John 8:12) is the source of life for every Believer. Jesus charged his followers to *"make disciples of all nations"*. (Matthew 28:19) Disciples are followers who replicate more followers who also replicate. We can only do so as we, like plant life to the sun, live in the power of His light. (Read I John 1:5-7) O, liberty-bearer, take hold of these freedoms while we have them to shine His light of truth in our land and throughout the world.

True freedom is a commodity that is meant to be exported, penetrating the darkened societies of the world, thus propagating cooperative nations that God uses to bless the world. This is the natural progression of freedom's light.

In 1831 Samuel Francis Smith wrote the beloved patriotic hymn, *'America'* and in one stanza wrote of the deep devotion the citizens of faith shared:

> *"Our father's God, to Thee,*
> *Author of liberty, to Thee we sing:*
> *'Long may our land be bright*
> *with freedom's holy light;*
> *protect us by Thy might,*
> *great God, our King!'"*

Such words should provoke us to the same action directed by the prophet Isaiah who wrote today's *five understandable words*:

> *"Arise, shine, for your light has come,*
> *and the glory of the LORD rises upon you."* (Isaiah 60:1)

It is both the duty and responsibility for patriots to continually remind the nation of such, while pointing those who do not share our worldview to the truth of God's light. Jesus taught that the light was not to be hidden, but to be set up high for all to enjoy its benefit. (Matthew 5:15)

The glory of the Lord rising upon the people is a way of saying that God's favor or blessings are a direct result of a people who do not shrink back from shining God's light: courageous people who not only embrace God's light, but allow it to shine through their lives at home, at work, at play, in government, and in travel. Those who do so will experience the favor and blessing of God. The Light of the world is foundational in the work of freedom.

> *"...where the Spirit*
> *of the Lord is,*
> *there is liberty."*
>
> 2 Corinthians 3:17

Pray for our country to follow the guiding light of God's truths and for our leaders to acknowledge the veracity of the sacred text.

"I . . . recommend a general and public return of praise and thanksgiving to Him from Whose goodness these blessings descend. The most effectual means of securing the continuance of our civil and religious liberties is always to remember with reverence and gratitude the Source from which they flow."

John Jay
Original Chief Justice
of
The Supreme Court

Source: William Jay, The Life of John Jay: With Selections From His Cor-respondence and Miscellaneous, to the Committee of the Corporation of the City of New York on June 29, 1826.

"...they will be my people..."

Jeremiah 24:7

God is explaining to Jeremiah the purpose of Israel's exile to Babylon. He showed Jeremiah two baskets of figs. When God asked Jeremiah what he saw before him, the prophet described the two baskets: one having ripe figs, perfect for consuming; the figs in the other basket were so rotten that they were only good to be thrown out. God then clarified that those exiled Israeli nationals would return and be as delightful in God's eyes as the ripe figs. However, Judah's King Zedekiah and his tribe, for their lack of faith and for their practice of religiosity represented the rotten figs. For those two things, the citizens of Judah would be refugees and would not be welcomed by anyone in the region.

Imagine for a moment having no connection, no belonging. Across this nation, there are towns and cities that provide healthy connections to their citizens. Of course, as the family goes, so goes the country... that's the essential connection for each person. God preserve and nourish the family in America!

When I was a child, the quickest and strongest connection that our family made after moving to a new community was through the local church. My mother was from the community and people could see my resemblance to her brothers. Just as the townspeople could tell whose child I was, so it is with the children of God. In fact, the world will know we are His disciples by our love for each other. (John 13:35)

The world should be able to see the distinct difference between the actions of God's children – children of light, and the actions of those who walk in darkness. (See Colossians 3) We are to be soldiers of light involved in an ongoing battle for the hearts and minds of living souls on this earth. God instructs us to be intentional in our love to all: our enemies, the sick, the downtrodden, those in prison, the hungry, the disenfranchised... everyone! The light in us is evidenced by the love through us.

Knowing **Whose** we are is foundational to how we exercise our freedoms. Thomas Jefferson understood the precept well. In his attempt at revealing the philosophy of Jesus, he quoted Jesus' teachings by cutting portions of texts from the Bible, and then arranged them on the

12

pages of a blank book which he sent to Secretary of Congress, Charles Thomson (who himself had published the 'Thomson's Bible' in 1808). In Jefferson's description of his creation, he stated:

"...a more beautiful or precious morsel of ethics I have never seen; it is a document in proof that I am a real Christian, that is to say, a disciple of the doctrines of Jesus."

Source: Randall, Henry S., *The Life of Thomas* Jefferson (NY: Derby and Jackson, 1958), Vol. 3, p. 451, Letter to Charles Thompson, January 9, 1816.

As you pray for the nation, ask God's Spirit to move across the land, turning hearts toward Him and His way, that all may know the sweet adoption of belonging to His eternal family.

"...the history of the Hebrew nation in all these respects—being the only truthful history ever written—was intended to teach the founders of other nations what foundations to lay, and the conservators and guardians of other nations what safeguards to insist on, in order that these nations might be successfully established, in order that they might be perpetuated to the latest generation of time."

J.E. Rankin, DD

Preached in the First Congregational Church, Washington, D.C., January 16th, 1876.

UNDERSTANDABLE 5 WORDS

"...I will be their God..."

Jeremiah 24:7

Many casual readers of Scripture may read this phrase and assume that because we are a free people, we are free to choose our focus of worship. To a large degree, we ARE free to do just so... AFTER first *rejecting* the One, true triune God found in the Father, Son, and Holy Spirit. The verse's progression reveals that we are first His. Only then does He become our aim of worship. We did not choose Him. Paul described it like this:

*"**He chose us in Him** before the foundation of the world, that we would be holy and blameless before Him. In love He predestined us to adoption as sons through Jesus Christ to Himself, according to the kind intention of His will."* (Ephesians 1:4-5, bold added for emphasis)

Paul explained this in a letter to the Roman Christians:

"And we know that God causes all things
to work together for good to those who love God,
to those who are called according to His purpose."
(Romans 8:28, bold added for emphasis)

We are chosen for the good works He has assigned us to do in bringing the light of His Kingdom to earth. (Read Ephesians 2:10)

Of course, the precept was first revealed in God's covenant with Abraham:

*"...the Lord your **God has chosen you** to be a*
people for His own possession..."
(Deuteronomy 7:6, bold added for emphasis)

It seems only natural that the Creator could lay claim to what is created. Don't you think? Have you ever baked a cake and had it rebel against you? Have you ever created a work plan, only for it to ignore the design for which it was created or talk back to you saying the plan won't work? Silly examples maybe, but they only show how ridiculous we are when we rebel and ignore God's plan for our lives.

God's heart breaks when we rebel and ignore His plan for our lives. He not only created us, He also purchased us through the blood of His Son, Jesus, that we might be doubly His through adoption. Jesus verified this precept when He taught His disciples:

> *"You did not choose Me but **I chose you**,*
> *and appointed you*
> *that you would go and bear fruit..."*
> (John 15:16, bold added for emphasis)

All of nature was affected by man's refusal to follow God's plan for our lives. (Genesis 3:17-19) The saddest thing found in all of God's creation is the signature of His creation despising their own Creator. The Bible tells us that rebellion is like witchcraft and it should not be in the life of a child of light. (I Samuel 15:23)

God, the Creator, has given us the freedom to respond to His calls of love – as we are made in His likeness, possessing independent thought and action. (Genesis 1:26) We are designed and created for a purpose, a heavenly purpose: to bring heaven to this world through the conduit of our lives. When God's love, mercy, and grace work in and through us, power is released on earth that makes an eternal difference in the lives of those we touch through our actions and words.

I am convinced that such was demonstrated by the pilgrims. Their motivating force was to be a people set apart for God's purposes:

> *"Having undertaken, for the glory of God,*
> *and advancement of the Christian faith..."*
> (The Mayflower Compact, paragraph two, line one).

Though these early settlers had sworn allegiance to England's King for protection and to establish commerce, their primary objective should be ours as well: that His Kingdom would come to earth as it is in heaven. This is true freedom when it is founded in and sustained by God. In fact, once they arrived in the new world, they began the colony under the auspices of self-government via majority rule of the townsmen; similar to the same approach modeled by the Virginia House of Burgesses.
(**Source:** www.pilgrimhallmuseum.org)

They lived as free people! There is no shame in declaring our allegiance to *"one nation, under God"*. (**Source:** our national pledge to the flag of The United States of America) The foundation of knowing **Whose** we are provides us the connection to what is eternal and true.

Thank God for His enduring love and grace as you pray for the nation today. Perhaps Psalm 136 will inspire your time in prayer. Reflect on your adoption into God's family and pray that your homeland to become "one nation under God".

"The great, vital, and conservative element in our system is the belief of our people in the pure doctrines and the divine truths of the Gospel of Jesus Christ"

Source: *Journal of the House of the Representatives of the United States of America* (Washington, DC: Cornelius Wendell, 1855), 34th Cong., 1st Sess., p. 354, January 23, 1856.

UNDERSTANDABLE 5 WORDS

"...*that they may serve Me.*"

Exodus 8:20

"...that they may serve Me."

Have you ever been impressed, truly impressed with the service you received at a restaurant? Did you notice that the server was not only accurate with the order, but that he or she took extra measures to assure: that your beverage was always topped off; that the quality of the food was up to your expectations; and that those in your party were satisfied? A good server has also prepared well: the table and place-settings are clean and neatly arranged; condiments stocked; and perhaps a decoration is appropriately placed to enhance the dining experience.

Perhaps all those things were done, but you were impressed with something greater... something greater *about* the person. Maybe it was his or her demeanor or the classy way the service was executed that convinced you this was no ordinary server.

A superior server does so with ease. An excellent waiter actually enjoys serving: takes pleasure in satisfying the customer; and relishes the reward of developing a relationship that will most certainly lead to a returning patron, thus improving the fiscal condition of the establishment. An outstanding attendant not only enjoys the role, but also reflects grace and deference to the customer without feeling in the least bit inferior. Such is the case for those who have died to self, living for the Redeemer.

A Christ-follower seeks to show those same qualities. After all, they were first demonstrated in Christ Himself. Paul describes such in his letter to the Philippian church:

"Who, being in very nature God,
did not consider equality with God
something to be used to His own advantage;
rather He made Himself nothing by taking the very nature of a servant,
being made in human likeness.
And being found in appearance as a man,
He humbled Himself by becoming obedient to death –
even death on a cross!"
(Philippians 2:5-11)

This Scripture explains how Christians are to treat each other by giving deference to each other rather than having a 'me first' attitude. Jesus' motivation was in the joy of those who would embrace His way and serve Him. (Hebrews 12:2) A day of joy is coming to all who serve the true Source of freedom, a day when we will sing of eternal freedom and celebrate its source!

Knowing Whose we are makes it crystal clear Who we serve, as in serving we give both tribute and honor. This foundation of freedom demonstrates our inability to sustain freedom and to lean upon His wisdom and power to do so.

"Our laws and our institutions must necessarily be based upon and embody the teachings of the Redeemer of mankind. It is impossible that it should be otherwise. In this sense, and to this extent, our civilizations and our institutions are emphatically Christian."

The Supreme Court of Illinois
1883

Source: Richmond v. Moore, 107 Ill. 429, 1883 WL 10319 (Ill.), 47 Am. Rep. 445 (Ill. 1883)

Pray for Godly people in positions of influence to provide righteous counsel to our leaders, providing discernment as they speak the truth in love.

UNDERSTANDABLE **5** WORDS

"...*this nation is your people.*"

Exodus 33:13

Israel had demonstrated her lack of trust in God's ways time and time again; so much so that God told Moses the entire nation risked annihilation from breaching the covenant God made with Abraham, Isaac, and Jacob. Then the reluctant leader who suffered from slow speech (Read Exodus, chapters 3-4) made a bold intercession for the nation. Moses reminded God that Israel was His chosen people. What a proclamation! It was true that they were stubborn; and, yes, they were also obstinate, but they were still God's chosen.

There is a document that is essential for any journey across national borders, it is called a passport. This certifies the person is a bona-fide citizen of its origin. With it, the citizen is granted certain privileges and restrictions for travel. If needed, the traveler may seek the embassy of their country for protection or counsel on international matters of government or business. Wherever one may go that passport identifies the traveler's origin and is essentially important for re-entry into one's homeland… it verifies to whom one belongs.

Moses was basically asking God to consider that each and every Israelite had their God-given passport to the Promised Land, holding God to His word. All the tribes living within that land shuddered at the thought of Israel's God Who goes before them assuring victory. Yet, God's own people struggled with this identity.

How could such be? How could a people who had been delivered from slavery, safely led through the Red Sea, and fed by God's hand with heavenly manna be a people that could still doubt and abandon the One Who had led them through the valley of the shadow of death?

What about Americans? How could we as a people turn our backs on the One Who raised this country into a lighthouse of liberty before the entire world? Why would even one generation think it wise to turn our backs on the Founder of Freedom that honored the backbone and determination of this country's founders?

It has recently been said by our country's leadership that we are no longer a Christian nation. This sad commentary is not a statement to be proud of, but one that should lead people of faith to their knees; and petition God to move across this land, turning hearts and minds back to His way of righteousness (*fair* and *accurate* in its exercise), and inspiring our leaders to demonstrate Godly leadership after the pattern of King David.

Let us affirm the high calling God has issued to:

> ➢ give honor to the Author of Liberty in our homes;
> ➢ revitalize our churches in our worship of the Prince of Peace;
> ➢ boldly sing the great songs that echo with the patriot's dream; and
> ➢ firm-up the foundations by prudent stewardship of our founding declarations.

Pray for a great revival across the land, where voices will once again echo the songs that give credit to the Author of Liberty; when churches will fill to overflowing with those seeking to receive guidance from the sacred text of God's word; and for those delivering sermons to accurately handle the word of truth.

*"...it is impossible
that any people of government
should ever prosper,
where men render
not unto God,
that which is God's,
as well as to Caesar,
that which is Caesar's."*
William Penn
Founder of Pennsylvania

Source: William Penn, Fundamental Constitutions of Pennsylvania, 1682.

"...plans I have for you..."

Jeremiah 29:11

The Author of History and Freedom breathed in each of us a desire that yearns to search for the script of freedom's story. We want to know the ending. Some people like to go to the end of a good book and read the ending before taking on the task of the journey in prose. Is desiring such unreasonable? Do we not give due diligence to research an investment before investing funds? We want to hedge our risk, or leverage our assets to produce the greatest dividend before expending funds.

God knows that we are as timid in the footsteps of faith as doubting Thomas, who had to see the nail scars before he would believe. (Read John 20:25) This is why God preserved these five simple words for us. They were written to a people in exile. God spoke through the prophet Jeremiah to those who had been exiled from the nation of Israel and displaced to Babylon. They were encouraged to make the best of the situation: to marry, have children, and to:

> *"...seek the welfare of the city*
> *where I have sent you into exile,*
> *and pray to the Lord on its behalf..."*
> (Jeremiah 29:7)

The weeping prophet then shared that God's 'plan' included seventy years of captivity, after which they would return to their homeland. (Read Jeremiah 29) God showed them the script, gave them the story's ending, and then gave the purpose for their captivity:

> *"'Then you will call upon Me and come and pray to Me,*
> *and I will listen to you.*
> *You will seek Me and find Me*
> *when you search for Me with all your heart.*
> *I will be found by you,' declares the Lord,*
> *'and I will restore your fortunes*
> *and will gather you from all the nations*
> *and from all the places where I have driven you,' declares the Lord,*
> *'and I will bring you back to the place from where I sent you into exile.'"*
> *(Jeremiah 29:12-14)*

God was instilling hope in their hearts when He inspired Jeremiah to write:

"'For I know the plans that I have for you,' declares the Lord, 'plans for welfare and not for calamity to give you a future and a hope.'"
(Jeremiah 29:11)

This would not be a permanent situation. God's calendar and timing are perfect for reflecting His sovereign rule and wisdom. We can trust Him to do the same for America while we seek to do everything in our power to let His love and light permeate a world darkened by corruption.

"There never has been a period in which the Common Law did not recognize Christianity as lying at its foundations."
Joseph Story

U. S. CONGRESSMAN; U.S. Supreme Court Justice; "FATHER OF AMERICAN JURISPRUDENCE".

Source: Joseph Story, *Life and Letters of Joseph Story*, William W. Story, editor , Vol. II, p. 8.

Pray for God's plans for our country, that we, once again, will be known as a people after His heart. Ask God to reveal what plans He has for your life to shine freedom's light in your community.

UNDERSTANDABLE 5 WORDS

"...be strong and

very courageous..."

Joshua 1:7

Joshua had been the commander of the entire Israeli army. Thousands upon thousands of men looked to him as their commander. For forty years Joshua had led them into battle and those men trusted him with their very lives. However, an essential part of the equation was suddenly missing… Moses was dead. The leader of leaders who had led Israel out of Egypt, through dry land across the Red Sea, receiving the Ten Commandments at Mount Sinai, and who interceded for a nation vacillating from devotion to desertion would not be there to walk upon the Promised Land with Joshua.

Before crossing the river, God spoke to Joshua, assuring him that just as He had been with Moses, so He would pledge Joshua's success for the rest of his life.

One might think Joshua didn't need such encouragement. God knew differently, for God searches the hearts and minds of men. (I Chronicles 28:9) God thought it so important that He demonstrated to Joshua His availability to be approached and to experience the personal counsel that Moses enjoyed for those many years.

The task ahead would still experience hurdles to be overcome: crossing the Jordan River; conquering the inhabitants of this Promised Land; making a journey around the city of Jericho each day for six days (and another seven trips on the seventh day); dividing the land; and establishing a new government for the nation known as the people of God. Doesn't sound like tasks for a timid leader.

Freedom is not made for the faint of heart. Freedom is only a reality when defined through the sacrifice of life by those who will not be constrained by any despot, and maintained by the blood of those who have enjoyed the benefits of freedom's veracity. Ask any people who have once been enslaved by some empirical rule and you will quickly discover that freedom and the quest for it builds strength, resolve, character, integrity, and hunger… a hunger to keep freedom strong and resolute against any threat of tyranny.

Any hint of risk to freedom must be met with resistance, for those who long for power in the quest for personal wealth or social control will seek to rob a nation of its independence and quench the songs of liberty - songs like our national anthem:

> *"O thus be it ever,*
> *when freemen shall stand*
> *Between their loved homes*
> *and the war's desolation.*
> *Blest with vict'ry and peace,*
> *may the Heav'n rescued land*
> *Praise the Power that hath made*
> *and preserved us a nation!*
> *Then conquer we must,*
> *when our cause it is just,*
> *And this be our motto:*
> *'In God is our trust.'*
> *And the Star - Spangled Banner*
> *in triumph shall wave*
> *O'er the land of the free*
> *and the home of the brave!"*
> (Francis Scott Key, September, 1814)

Being strong and courageous is essential in securing a nation's liberty. Fly the nation's colors boldly this day and give thanks to the One Who preserved our independence. *Be strong and very courageous* in maintaining a government by the people, for the people under God's banners of truth and righteousness.

Pray for leaders of free nations to possess the strengths of: discernment to comprehend the complexities of contemporary issues; courage to stand for truth; wisdom to develop the proper course of action that will shine with the eternal truths upon which our forefathers depended. Perhaps Psalm 115 will encourage your prayer time.

UNDERSTANDABLE **5** WORDS

"The Lord is my strength…"

Exodus 15:2

"The Lord is my strength…"

A miracle of unforeseen proportions had just occurred: the entire nation of one million people had just crossed a vast sea through a corridor of liquid walls, walking on dry ground, and safely arriving on the other side to witness the destruction of a hostile army seeking to destroy them… and they never lifted a finger against them. I'm sure it left many of them scratching their heads in disbelief at the sequence of events that had just occurred. (Read Exodus 14)

Imagine having lived your whole life in servitude and experiencing a rescue on so great a scale that you know it could only have happened by the hand of God. And for the first time in your life you sense freedom. The air seems fresher. Your limbs feel stronger.

The family celebrates the joy of independence from centuries of oppression. In fact, the celebration began when Moses was inspired to write a new song! He then taught the song to others and it quickly spread throughout the camps of the nation rising into a glorious reprise of a national chorus giving credit to Whom credit is due, the Lord of Hosts, the God of Israel, the Great I Am, Jehovah God.

Freedom comes at such great cost, and these people honored the generations who had paid the price in slavery. They hoped for a savior and for their nation to once again know the blessed favor of being free to work, build, buy, sell, grow, tend, love, and worship.

Freedom always leads to great songs of deliverance and thanksgiving, and this time was no different. This new song of praise and thanks peers into the wonder of liberation. Having been rescued from such hostile and insidious conditions, a dinner of fish by the Red Sea with one's family while singing the new national anthem is all that a mind was able to comprehend for one day.

Victory songs ring with confidence in God, even our own:

> *"I have seen Him in the watch-fires of*
> *a hundred circling camps,*
> *They have builded Him an altar*
> *in the evening dews and damps;*

"The Lord is my strength…"

I can read His righteous sentence
by the dim and flaring lamps:
His day is marching on."
(Julia Ward Howe, November, 1861)

His truth is indeed marching on and its light will not be extinguished. Let that knowledge embolden each of us with renewed strength to give credit to Whom credit is due. Within the foundation of freedom are the songs of deliverance and celebration in recognizing God's divine hand coming to the rescue of those who were once conquered or enslaved.

As you come before God today, pray with thanksgiving for the hand of God that intervened in the course of history for our nation to be birthed and established as one nation, under God. Consider praying through Psalm 112 as your offering of thanksgiving.

*"The great pillars of all govern-
ment and of social life [are] virtue,
morality, and religion. This is the
armor, my friend, and this alone,
that renders us invincible."*

Patrick Henry

Source: Patrick Henry, *Patrick Henry: Life, Correspondence and Speeches*,
William Wirt Henry, editor; to Archibald Blair on January 8, 1799.

UNDERSTANDABLE 5 WORDS

"So David blessed the Lord..."

I Chronicles 29:10

All national leaders want to leave their mark on the pages of history. Every president, king, pharaoh, premier, tsar, or prime minister wants to know how his/her life will be measured through the scales of time and perpetuity. Today's *five understandable words* display David's efforts to galvanize how he would be remembered.

David had contributed great amounts of his personal wealth to erect a lasting tribute. However, this landmark had nothing to do with preserving David's legacy. Instead, the shepherd turned king was constructing a tribute to the Source of Freedom for the nation Israel. David wanted all the tribute and honor going to God. He even passed the blueprints to his son, Solomon, to complete after his death. (Read 1 Chronicles 28)

A national call for more resources was issued with overwhelming results of the Israeli people following the king's lead. It was at that point when David, so inspired by the outpouring of faith exhibited by the people, worshiped God:

"Blessed are You,
O Lord God of Israel our father,
forever and ever.
Yours, O Lord, is the greatness
and the power and the glory
and the victory
and the majesty,
indeed everything that is in
the heavens and the earth;
Yours is the dominion, O Lord,
and You exalt Yourself as head over all.
Both riches and honor come from You,
and You rule over all,
and in Your hand is power and might;
and it lies in Your hand to make great
and to strengthen everyone.
Now therefore, our God,
we thank You,
and praise Your glorious name. "
(I Chronicles 29:10-13)

Pray that all nations will have leaders with the faith and the backbone to demonstrate such dependence on God's favor and such devotion to lead in the worship of our God Who saves. Praying for one's country should never cease before making intercession for the leaders of free people around the world. Seek God's face today as you stand in the gap, offering intercession for those influencing political leaders. Pray David's prayer out loud as you stand in the gap for our leaders.

After George Washington's inauguration, the presidential address was given in Federal Hall (NYC) where Washington demonstrated a similar dependence on God's favor. The text can be found at the end of this vignette. A founding principle of liberty is seen and heard in the leaders of free nations who acknowledge the Author of Freedom. God, bless free countries with leaders after Your heart.

"... it would be peculiarly impro-per to omit in this first official act my fervent supplications to that Almighty Being Who rules over the universe, Who presides in the councils of nations, and Whose providential aids can supply every human defect – that His bene-diction may consecrate to the liberties and happiness of the people of the United States a government instituted by them-selves for these essential purposes."

George Washington

Source: The Debates and Proceedings in the Congress of the United States, Joseph Gales, editor , Vol. I, p. 27.

UNDERSTANDABLE 5 WORDS

"...magnify the Lord with me..."
Psalm 34:3

Here is found the sweetest invitation to enjoy the communion of fellow Believers. This call by Israel's king to worship together is a picture of a leader whose strength is not in the polls, not in the vote of the people, but in God and God alone. David's love for God and His way united a nation fragmented by exile and domination in the singular truth of being God's chosen people.

David's profession of devotion to God prepared the hearer's ears for the invitation:

> *"I will bless the Lord at all times;*
> *His praise shall continually be in my mouth.*
> *My soul will make its boast in the Lord;*
> *the humble will hear it and rejoice."*
> (Psalm 34:1-2)

Does this mean that every citizen rallied to this clarion call of worship? Probably not, though David did not let that dissuade him from being the leader God had called him to be, and that included leading people to the throne of God's grace. David's determination to influence others toward faith in God is also reflected in Psalm 20:7, *"Some trust in chariots and some in horses, but we trust in the name of the Lord our God."* (ESV)

Our founding fathers were just as courageous to speak of their trust in God for their appointments in history. Historical revisionists purport that the Founders were deists who marginalized Christianity. However, the words they left us seem to paint a different picture. The evidence points to a people of great faith. That faith shaped their worldview and the principles by which they lived. Two great examples are found in the words of Benjamin Franklin and Daniel Webster. The aged Franklin stated:

"I have lived, Sir, a long time, and the longer I live, the more convincing proofs I see of this truth, that God governs in the affairs of men.

And if a sparrow cannot fall to the ground without His notice, is it probable that an empire can rise without His aid? We have been assured, Sir, in the Sacred Writings, that 'except the Lord build the House, they labor in vain that build it.' I firmly believe this; and I also believe that without His concurring aid we shall succeed in this political building no better than the builders of Babel: We shall be divided by our partial local interests; our projects will be confounded, and we ourselves shall become a reproach and bye word down to future ages."

Benjamin Franklin

(**Source:** Benjamin Franklin, *The Writings of Benjamin Franklin*, Jared Sparks, editor (Boston: Tappan, Whittemore and Mason, 1840), Vol. X, p. 297, April 17, 1787.)

Mr. Webster provided his perspective:

"…let us not forget the religious character of our origin. Our fathers were brought hither by their high veneration for the Christian religion. They journeyed by its light and labored in its hope. They sought to incorporate its principles with the ele-

ments of their society, and to diffuse its influence through all their institutions, civil, political, or literary. Let us cherish these sentiments, and extend this influence still more widely; in the full conviction, that that is the happiest society which partakes in the highest degree of the mild and peaceful spirit of Christianity." **Daniel Webster**

Source: Daniel Webster, The Works of Daniel Webster, 1851, Vol. I.

Will you pray for patriots of today to recognize this heritage and preserve its value? Echo Psalm 103 as you remember our righteous origin.

UNDERSTANDABLE **5** WORDS

"...fools despise wisdom and instruction."

Proverbs 1:7

Solomon is revealing his purpose statement in the first nine verses of Proverbs. He used this collection of wisdom to teach the young boys in the Judaic schools how to acquire, use, and keep wisdom, as well as the benefits wisdom brings to both the individual and a nation. He was preparing the next generation.

Light exposes those whose deeds are done in darkness – those who grew up despising wisdom and instruction in righteousness. Psalm 14:1 tells us that the fool does not believe in God's existence. In other words, there are those whose very core of understanding is without the hope of heaven; without the enjoyment of knowing God's favor; without His comfort in times of grief; without the power to overcome difficulties; and without the wisdom of His Spirit.

The one who says in his heart there is no God is bound to be part of history's equation to repeat itself, making the same mistakes again and again. Without God's presence our minds are darkened to the benefits of His Word and His Way.

The apostle Paul wrote of the obvious disparity between those who walk in darkness and those who walk in God's light:

"For you were once darkness, but now you are light in the Lord. Live as children of light (for the fruit of the light consists in all goodness, righteousness and truth) and find out what pleases the Lord. Have nothing to do with the fruitless deeds of darkness, but rather expose them." (Ephesians 5:5-12)

Since the renaissance, enlightenment has long been lauded. Jesus Himself spoke of the enlightenment that He brought into the world:

"I am the light of the world.
Whoever follows me will never walk in darkness,
but will have the light of life."
(John 8:12)

He did not say that He would enlighten others or point them to enlightenment. He stated that He Himself is the light. As the embodiment of truth, Jesus leads His followers by His own light into His righteous and perfect way.

O sojourner, do not despise the way of blessing. Seek His instruction and gain wisdom for living. Katharine Lee Bates penned the now beloved words to the patriotic hymn, *'America the Beautiful'*. The third stanza speaks of citizens who realize the blessing found in sound wisdom and instruction, namely self-control and living under the law:

> *"America, America,*
> *God mend thine ev'ry flaw;*
> *Confirm thy soul in self-control,*
> *thy liberty in law."*

Our liberty, our freedom, is found in embracing the truth of instruction and applying it wisely toward self-control. This is the blessing of a free society and a powerful tool to use in preserving our freedoms and enlightening other nations.

Foundational, then, to our freedom are the efforts made by citizens to research, understand, and synthesize the source, dynamics, constraints, and flexibilities of the liberties we know. The Founders certainly knew the source of their liberty in developing our founding documents. Samuel Adams described freedom's source as:

"...imprinted by the finger of God
on the heart of man."

Source: Samuel Adams, The Writings of Samuel Adams, Henry Alonzon Cushing, editor; "to the Legislature of Massachusetts", January 17, 1794.

Are you praying for those in your circle of influence to hear and know the voice of God and the truths of His Word?

"...wisdom that leads

to salvation..."

2 Timothy 3:15

Paul is writing young Timothy to warn him of perilous times and evil men who *"have a form of godliness"*. (2 Timothy 3:5) We know that for every good thing God provides, satan seeks to have a confederate or imitation to substitute in its place. The apostle Paul instructed the Corinthian church that the wisdom of this age *"comes to nothing"*. He explained that human wisdom is juxtaposed to the wisdom from God (the Spirit). (Read I Corinthians 2:6-16)

Many actions have occurred in the name of Christianity: actions that in no way mirror the love and grace of Jesus Christ. The Bible tells us that God is the provider of wisdom and if anyone lacks it, all one needs to do is ask and He will supply it. (James 1:5-7) The wisdom of God leads to salvation whereas the wisdom of the world will give every possible excuse to turn souls away from the truth of God's salvation through His Son, Jesus Christ. The world sees such as foolishness (Read 2 Corinthians 2:14), but the Christ follower sees it as God's display of power through the change in a life. (1 Corinthians 1:18)

A college professor of mine cited Karl Marx as stating, *"Religion is the sigh of the oppressed creature… It is the opium of the people."* It may be so. I'm not trying to quibble. However, religion in its strictest definition as 'a particular *system* of faith practice is quite different from the *relationship* Jesus invited His followers to pursue. Though the founders used the term in their day, it did not carry the same meaning as today. In their day, 'religion' was the relationship with God in following the doctrines and life of Jesus Christ.

Religion as a particular system of religious exercise is merely man's attempt to achieve eternal rewards based on personal performance and, as such, may then be the opium of the people - a self-centered people (a counterfeit to the relationship God desires with every person). A relationship with Jesus Christ is based on His redemptive work on the cross. Paul described it this way to the Ephesian church:

"For it is by grace you have been saved, through faith – and this is not from yourselves, it is the gift of God – not by works, so that no one can boast (in one's own works). *For we are God's handiwork, created in*

Christ Jesus to do good works, which God prepared in advance for us to do. (Ephesians 2:8-9; words in parenthesis added for clarity)

Godly wisdom is what is needed for free nations to both survive and flourish. Godly wisdom does indeed lead to salvation for a person, a community, and a nation. Such wisdom will be the saving grace that keeps a nation from destroying itself through corruption, greed, misuse of power, injustice, and the like. Godly wisdom is the use of knowledge in a way that will give credit and honor to God.

Samuel Smith's beautiful tribute, *'America'* encourages the masses in this way:

> *"Our glorious land today,*
> *'neath education's sway,*
> *soars upward still.*
> *Its hills of learning fair,*
> *whose bounties all may share,*
> *behold them everywhere*
> *on vale and hill!"*

The bounties Smith described were the golden nuggets of truth found in God's Word. Such knowledge leads to salvation as described by Jesus:

> *"You will know the truth and the*
> *truth will set you free."*
> (John 8:32)

What could be more foundational? O, patriot, work hard to learn the everlasting truths of God's Word that can be heralded freely through our school systems and not be censored by those espousing the world's wisdom. The exercise of Godly wisdom will help preserve our freedom for generations to come.

Let's join in collective prayers for our educational system to once again point to the Founders' source of inspiration for independence. Will you pray as a soldier of light against the opiates of contemporary societies – pornography, post-modernism, etc.

"Before our children remove their religious connections... before they leave the old paths of God's Word... before they barter their birthright for a mess of pottage – let us place in their hands this chronicle of the glorious days of the suffering Churches, and let them know that they are the sons of the men 'of whom the world was not worthy', and whose sufferings for conscience are here monumentally recorded."

Source: John Overton Choules, August 12, 1843, in the Preface to the 1844 reprint of Daniel Neal's, "History of the Puritans", 1731.

"…be strong in the grace that is in Christ Jesus.
The things which you
have heard from me
in the presence of many witnesses,
entrust these to faithful men
who will be able
to teach others also…"

2 Timothy 2:1-2

"Those who love Your law..."

Psalm 119:165

"Those who love Your law..."

Psalm 119:165

UNDERSTANDABLE 5 WORDS

"Those who love Your law..."

Psalm 119:165

There are two hidden promises for those who love God's Word:

- ➢ Great peace
- ➢ Discernment

Notice the first part of the promise is quantified; it promises **great** peace, not some appearance of peace in a politically correct environment to appease power brokers behind the scenes. Great peace shows faith and trust in a great God. When we place our lives in the hands of the One Who created the universe there is both confidence and peace.

We can know that,

> *"...all things work together for the good to those who love Him..."*
> (Romans 8:28)

Now, that is confident peace!

Discernment is like turning on a light – it keeps one from stumbling over the personal obstacles of compromise and prejudice. In other words, we will not get in God's way from completing His purpose for our lives, once unknown when we lived as children of darkness. Now that we are children of light, we have been exposed to God's way and have been enlightened to the benefits of freedom with responsibility. It is essential that workers of freedom seek to understand the worldview of nations oppressed through totalitarianism, despotism, socialism, and the like. These worldviews have not yet seen the light of freedom's dividends both practically and spiritually. Once we understand their worldview, we are better equipped to pray through the barriers preventing the spread of God's freedom.

Practically speaking we can embrace 'the law' for its benefits:

- God is the one true God – no other gods = no confusion.
- God will not share His glory to a man-made idol - ditto.
- God wants us to respect His name – teaches respect.
- God designed a Sabbath rest for man to rest – we all need it.
- God promises a longer life when we honor our parents.

- God prohibits the taking of human life – establishing the sanctity of life.
- God prohibits adultery – protecting individuals, marriages, and families.
- God prohibits stealing – ensuring integrity in business and security of one's belongings.
- God prohibits making false statements against others – preserving personal reputations.
- God wants us to be content with our life – things work better.
  (Exodus 20)

God's law exposes us to the reality of sin and how it separates us from a holy God. (see Romans 7:7; Galatians 3:19) If it were not for the law, we would not have a conscious awareness of our need for a savior. Since we could not meet every letter of the law, Christ took the consequence for such and we, who deserve judgment, are justified fully through the atoning work of Christ on the cross.

God's law is meant to protect us from sabotaging our relationship with Him and with others. He made each of us and understands us better than anyone else. He desires our lives to be connected, unhindered by the barriers unrighteous behavior brings into relationships.

When we seek His way, we will have peace in the midst of the turmoil in this world. Jesus put it this way:

> *"These things I have spoken to you,*
> *so that in Me you may have peace.*
> *In the world you have tribulation,*
> *but take courage;*
> *I have overcome the world."*
> (John 16:33)

This is why we should cherish the Word of God all the more for pricking our conscience with the awareness of right and wrong, and pointing us to freedom from the prison of sin. Let freedom ring against enslavement either by men or by sin!

Foundational to true freedom is love for God's law and His Word of life that brings freedom's benefits. **Our prayers to elevate the benefits of lawful living can and will make a difference. Pray that the rule of law in free countries will be established and respected.**

"The moment the idea is admitted into society that property is not sacred as the laws of God and that there is not a force of law and public justice to protect it, anarchy and tyranny commence. If 'Thou shalt not covet,' and 'Thou shalt not steal,' were not commandments of Heaven, they must be made inviolable precepts in every society, before it can be civilized or made free."

Source: John Adams, *The Works of John Adams; Vol. VI, p. 9.*

UNDERSTANDABLE 5 WORDS

"*You shall teach them diligently...*"

Deuteronomy 6:7

The desert became the college for the nation of Israel. It was during the forty years they wandered in the desert that God taught His chosen people the precepts of faith. Why would a people who saw the plagues and the parting of the Red Sea need lessons in faith? The Israelites offended God at the base of Mount Sinai when they demanded that Aaron fashion an idol for worship (Read Exodus 32:1-10), in defiance of the second commandment they would soon receive. (Exodus 20:4-5)

The forty years of wandering were part of the judgment God gave the nation, causing an entire generation to die off. God instructed Moses that His commandment should be diligently taught to the nation's children. The central commandment given was:

> *"You shall love the Lord your God*
> *with all your heart,*
> *and with all your soul and with all your might."* (Deuteronomy 6:5)

Though this was the principle command, they were also to matriculate through a complete understanding of the Ten Commandments. It must have become painfully clear that God takes the business of righteousness very seriously. God wanted His chosen to be a good people, reflecting His virtues of goodness, fairness and excellence (*righteousness*).

Each parent was commanded to memorize the law and be intimately familiar with it. (Deuteronomy 6:6) The mandate set before them was to teach their children well. It began in the classroom of the home.

Verse six is actually translated, *"shall be on your heart"*; that's where we get the expression to 'know something by heart'. It is when we are that familiar with a body of knowledge that we become experts in both its scope and sequence. The children of Israel were in classrooms with the finest teachers of the world: their own parents.

The direction to teach the laws to the children came with a qualifying description on how the children were to be taught. This was not to be a casual conversation where one gives a nod to God with the wink of an eye. It was to be taught diligently, with persistent personal attention.

God even described how the teaching would occur:

"…talk of them when you sit in your house and when you walk by the way and when you lie down and when you rise up. You shall bind them as a sign on your hand and they shall be as frontals on your forehead. You shall write them on the doorposts of your house and on your gates."
(Deuteronomy 6:7-9)

There was to be no misunderstanding the basis for the new *free* nation. The moral absolutes had to be established for the nation to be administered justly and for their judicial system to work properly. In this manner, people would assimilate God's moral law, not as someone's opinion, but as God's prerequisite for staying free. Taking God's Word out of education's standards and the basis for civil law removes a foundational element of liberty.

The home is the primary teaching center for conveying the truths of God's Word, and the classroom should complement these precepts through further study and application for young minds developing their moral compasses.

In 1833, Noah Webster published an edition of The Holy Bible in the Common Version with amendments of the language (to give words not commonly known at the time suitable substitutes for the people of his day to encourage understanding and the continued reading of God's Word). In the forward, Webster describes the Bible as *"the chief moral cause of all that is good, and the best corrector of all that is evil in human society"*. As a founder, Webster was pointing his fellow citizens to the Word to be read and taught in the home! (**Source:** Webster, Noah, *The Holy Bible in the Common Version with Amendments of the Language*; 1833)

The prayers of parents for their children must be so precious to the Giver of Life; the prayers by a community for its families are just as precious! Likewise, present your local school administrators and teachers before our Lord for His guidance and for our schools to once again present the benefits of a righteous society.

" The Bible... should be read in our schools in preference to all other books because it contains the greatest portion of that kind of knowledge which is calculated to produce private and public happiness."

Benjamin Rush

Source: Benjamin Rush, *Essays, Literary, Moral and Philosophical*, 1798, pp. 94, 100, "A Defence of the Use of the Bible as a School Book."

"…but seek first

His kingdom…"

Matthew 6:33

While teaching on the side of a mountain, Jesus contrasted those who are religious with those who desire intimacy with God. Jesus taught that when we walk with God our needs will be met, and in that instruction, the multitude was encouraged to put God's Kingdom first on their life's priority list.

The world, however, puts great credence in the systems created by man. Educator Benjamin Bloom developed a chart of the hierarchy of learning in educational philosophy:

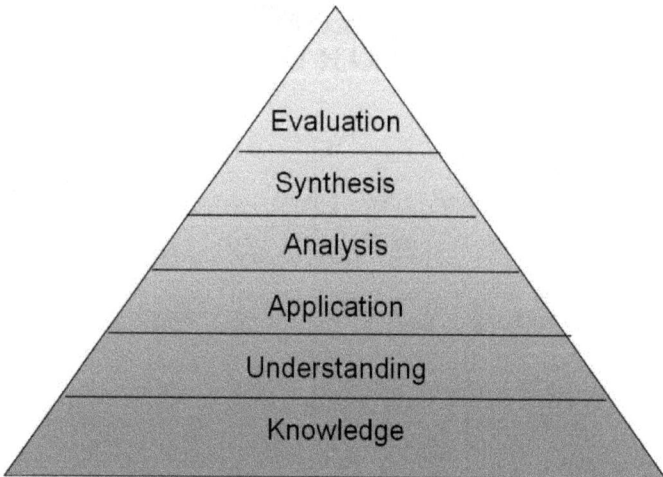

Working up the pyramid, Bloom shows the process of learning facts to which understanding is added, then applied. Maturity then analyzes and synthesizes information by applying knowledge to related areas. Finally, accuracy in the handling of knowledge occurs when one is able to evaluate its effectiveness. **(Source:** Bloom, B.S., Engelhart, M.D., Furst, E.J., Hill, W.H., Krathwuhl, D.R., *Taxonomy of Educational Objectives*: The Classification of Educational Goals (NY: David McKay, Co.), 1956.

The basics of reading, writing, and arithmetic, however, are not enough to know and preserve the freedoms we enjoy. God's Word instructs us to seek the things of His Kingdom that we may be fully versed in the ways of righteous living in order to demonstrate both strength and grace.

Peter described a spiritual progression in his second letter to the first century churces. In his hierarchy of development he gives a promise that when proper attention is given to spiritual disciplines, one would never be found ineffective or unproductive. He wrote:

> *"...make every effort to*
> *add to your faith, goodness;*
> *and to goodness, knowledge;*
> *and to knowledge, self-control;*
> *and to self-control, perseverance;*
> *and to perseverance, Godliness;*
> *and to Godliness, mutual affection;*
> *and to mutual affection, love."*
> (2 Peter 1:5-7)

Notice that knowledge is listed third. In God's economy knowledge is not first, faith is; for it is impossible to please God – except through faith. (Hebrews 11:6) Where do we get the faith? The Bible explains that Jesus is the Author and Perfecter of our faith. (Hebrews 12:2)

There is a sound reason to have knowledge listed after faith and goodness. Faith demonstrates our inability to save ourselves or impact others. Goodness demonstrates our understanding that we are in this experience of life together. Without these two qualities knowledge will only bloat a person with pride which only places walls between people. Paul put it this way:

> *"... knowledge puffs up while love builds up."*
> (I Corinthians 8:1)

When we prioritize God's Kingdom, we are surrendering our preferences, our prejudices, our own biases, and our worldview to His. Our worldview can be filled with prejudice and hatred of every kind. Our preferences can be so egocentric that we lose sight of God's plan and purpose for our lives – the good works He has planned for us to do, revealing His Kingdom on earth. (Ephesians 2:9)

"...but seek first His kingdom..."

When we place our first priority on developing faith, goodness, knowledge, self-control, perseverance, Godliness, mutual affection, and love to be used for and by our Savior, then the prayer He taught us to pray will come to be:

"Your Kingdom come, Your will be done, on earth as it is in heaven."
(Matthew 6:10)

Jesus wanted those on earth to experience heaven's hope and liberty. There can be no freedom apart from that true freedom given by God, the Author of freedom.

Pray for hearts to be reached, eyes to be opened, and minds to embrace the eternal truths of God's good and righteous Kingdom.

"...the only means of establishing and perpetuating our republican forms of government is the universal education of our youth in the principles of Christianity by means of the Bible."

Source: Rush, Benjamin, *Essays, Literary, Moral & Philosphical* 1798, p. 112, "A Defense of the Use of the Bible as a School Book."

UNDERSTANDABLE **5** WORDS

"...then you will have success..."

Joshua 1:8

Just as the pilgrims fled to America for freedom to worship, so many others saw opportunity for personal advancement by establishing new avenues of commerce in raw materials through exporting and importing, real estate, defense, etc. From the start of the new experiment for freedom there have been those who positioned themselves at the forefront to leverage their timing and expertise toward personal gain.

Success is measured in a plethora of paradigms awarding achievement for expertise in specialized areas or abilities, societal improvement, medical breakthroughs, education, business, innovation, etc. Bessie Anderson Stanley's poetic description of success has been lauded by many:

"He has achieved success who has lived well, laughed often, and loved much; who has enjoyed the trust of pure women, the respect of intelligent men and the love of little children; who has filled his niche and accomplished his task; who has left the world better than he found it, whether an improved poppy, a perfect poem, or a rescued soul; who has always looked for the best in others and given the best he had; whose life was an inspiration; whose memory a benediction."
Source: *Heart Throbs, Volume Two* [ed. Joseph Mitchell Chappell] (Boston: Chappel Pub. Co., 1911), pp. ii, 1-2.

I remember a history teacher crediting Thomas Edison for stating that success was one percent inspiration and ninety-nine percent perspiration. Today's five understandable words are found in God's instruction to Joshua on true success:

> *"This book of the law shall not*
> *depart from your mouth,*
> *but you shall meditate on it day and night,*
> *so that you may be careful to do*
> *according to all that is written in it;*
> *for then you will make your way prosperous,*
> *and **then you will have success.**"*
> (Joshua 1:8, bold added for emphasis)

In God's economy, success is in our reach as we walk in the light and favor of the One Who is for us. The Bible states: *"If God is for us who can be against us?"* (Romans 8:31) Paul reinforced this precept when he instructed the Philippians in this way: *"I can do all things through Christ Who strengthens me."* (Philippians 4:13)

Centuries earlier, King David taught his son, Solomon:

> *"Keep the charge of the LORD your God,*
> *to walk in His ways,*
> *to keep His statutes,*
> *His commandments,*
> *His ordinances, and*
> *His testimonies,*
> *according to what is written in the Law of Moses,*
> *that you may succeed in all that you do and wherever you turn..."*
> (I Kings 2:3)

Solomon must have listened to his father's advice, using it in the literature he developed for teaching in the Hebrew schools of that day. (Proverbs 3:1-4) And it should be taught: handed down from one generation to the next, which is exactly what David did with his son, Solomon. King David even declared such to be recorded for antiquity: *"One generation commends your works to another; they tell of Your mighty acts."* (Psalm 145:4)

In her beautiful description of the source for America's success, Katherine Lee Bates wrote a beloved patriotic hymn, *'America the Beautiful'*:

> *"America, America,*
> *may God thy gold refine*
> *till all success be nobleness*
> *and ev'ry gain divine."*

71

Let freedom ring throughout the land that all America's gains point to a heavenly origin. This facet of *Freedom's Foundation* reveals success as founded upon the precepts of the sacred texts.

Pray for the success of free nations who have embraced the God's paradigm for freedom. Pray for Christian business men and women to acknowledge God and His way as credit for their success.

UNDERSTANDABLE 5 WORDS

"Nations will come to you..."

Isaiah 60:3

Growing up in the south, I was exposed to the term: 'company's comin''. And whenever we were expecting company (visiting friends or family):

- ➤ The house was thoroughly cleaned.
- ➤ Favorite foods were prepared.
- ➤ Everyone dressed nicer.
- ➤ Only the best behavior was expected.

Needless to say, it was a special time to display our best to our guests. However, the Bible teaches that guests will come on a national level when the host nation reflects God's ways of *fairness and accuracy* (righteousness). A country that espouses righteous acts and demonstrates such in her laws and policies will enjoy the admiration of a watching world. The world will see how righteousness infects a society with integrity in business, strength in the family, decency in one's personal life, resolve in both personal and national responsibilities, duty in protecting our way of living, and compassion for those in need. (Read Matthew 5:14-16)

The Democratic National Convention of 1968 met at the Hilton Hotel in downtown Chicago. On the third day of the convention anti-war demonstrators began gathering outside the hotel. By evening, police arrived in overwhelming numbers to break up the protesters. As they brandished their riot gear, tear gas, and began maneuvers to disperse the mob, the crowd began to chant: *"The whole world is watching."* This chant became the theme of a generation searching for meaning and significance in the midst of a society gone awry. It seemed that the righteousness – which intrigued nations to admire our republic – had disappeared from the American landscape, evidenced by the harassment and harm the protesters received from fellow citizens.

The world is watching America today to see if she will drift even further from the moorings of her origins or once again shine strong as a nation that holds to the anchor of righteousness. Let this ingredient in *Freedom's Foundation* once again act as a lighthouse guiding nations into the port of freedom's safety. **Will you pray for those who are visiting our nation in our schools and businesses to be introduced to God's liberty?**

"*Let us enter on this important business under the idea that we are Christians on whom the eyes of the world are now turned... let us earnestly call and beseech Him... to preside in our councils... We can only depend on the all powerful influence of the Spirit of God, Whose Divine aid and assistance it becomes us as a Christian people most devoutly to implore.*"

Elias Boudinot

PRESIDENT OF CONGRESS; SIGNED THE PEACE TREATY TO END THE AMERICAN REVOLUTION; FIRST ATTORNEY ADMITTED TO THE U. S. SUPREME COURT BAR; FRAMER OF THE BILL OF RIGHTS; DIRECTOR OF THE U. S. MINT

Source: Elias Boudinot, *The Life, Public Services, Addresses, and Letters of Elias Boudinot*, Vol. I, pp. 19, 21.

UNDERSTANDABLE 5 WORDS

"...the nations

will be blessed..."

Galatians 3:18

"...the nations will be blessed..."

These *five understandable words* are found within the gentle correction Paul gave to the Galatian church. They had become legalists by adding conditions for new converts to be accepted within the fellowship. (See Acts 15; Galatians 2) The point Paul was making referred to Abraham being counted righteous by God on the basis of his faith alone, not by any tradition or works on his part.

Paul, a converted Jew who had been well-schooled in Judaic law and history, explained that *the nations will be blessed* through the seed of Abraham and explained that seed to be Jesus Christ. The blessing then comes through the expression of God to us through the life, death, and resurrection of His Son, Jesus Christ.

Our nation blesses other nations with nutritional, medical, technical, and military aid in times of distress. However, a social gospel without the power of the cross is nothing but a clanging cymbal. (See I Corinthians 13:1-3) Just as freedom is meant to be exported, propagated, or spread to the farthest reaches of the earth, so the source for that freedom is to be dispersed among all peoples, all tribes, and all nations. On the day Jesus ascended to heaven, he directed His disciples to:

> *"...go, and make disciples of all nations..."* (Matthew 28:19).

The call of Christ is a call to go. Jesus prepared His disciples for such when He sent them out by pairs. He described what they would experience:

> *"I send you out as sheep*
> *in the midst of wolves..."*
> (Matthew 10:19)

It doesn't sound like they were heading into friendly territory. It is well known that eventually all but John and Judas were martyrs for the call of Christ. John was exiled to the island of Patmos between modern day Greece and Turkey. Judas committed suicide after betraying Jesus in the garden. (See Revelation 1:9; Matthew 27:5)

Our call to bless all nations with the good news of God's love and the benefits that come with following His way should stand in stark contrast to the world's systems. Many point to the dark ages and the massacres by Christian crusaders as an indictment on anyone who bears the name of the Prince of Peace. However, a serious student of history need only to discover five hundred years of death and oppressive rule by another people whose worldview is quite different from our own: a worldview that continues to this day, creating a clash of cultures that justifies horrendous actions.

Yes, it is true that the finger can be pointed at Christians who justified similar acts through the misuse of biblical interpretation: namely, those who continued the practice of slavery, prejudice, and hatred toward people of color. We still witness the continuing struggle in our streets across America; a conflict that originated from the consequences of actions by Americans three hundred years ago.

If the nations are to once again be blessed by our worldview, we must get past this serious threat to our country. Reconciliation *can* happen by united people committed to shining God's light.

As Jesus was preparing the disciples for His departure, he explained that worse than the prisons of this world is the bondage of sin. The blessing God extends to all people is the freedom from that bondage. Jesus had already instructed his followers that the truth would make them free. Of course, He was referring to Himself as the embodiment of truth, the Living Word that became flesh. (See John 8:32; John 1:1-14)

Jesus explained that when one embraces Him as Savior, there is real freedom: *"If the son makes you free, you will be free indeed..."* (John 8:36) This is the greatest blessing to impart to the nations of the world, and our forefathers embraced the idea as foundational to the existence of the country they birthed.

Let us pray for messengers to share the good news of this freedom. Perhaps pray how God would use you in delivering this message to a world longing for freedom.

> *"Suppose a nation in some distant region should take the Bible for their only law book and every member should regulate his conduct by the precepts there exhibited. . . . What a Eutopia – what a Paradise would this region be!"*

John Adams

Second president of the United States, signer of the Declaration of Independence, and one of the two signers of the Bill of Rights

Source: Adams, *Works*, Vol. II, pp. 6-7, diary entry for February 22, 1756.

"Go into all the world..."

Matthew 20:20

Jesus' command to infiltrate the world with the message of His life given for the forgiveness of sins was not for a single generation or assigned just to the disciples. The marching order for all followers of Christ is to go and tell. The more accurate translation for *"Go"* is, 'As you are going' – it is a continuous action that implies being intentional in every facet of our lives. We cannot pigeon hole our faith to a Sunday activity; it must be evident in every waking moment.

There is another criterion though that Jesus gave… one that causes many Christians to squirm when reading the passage: *"into all the world"*. This does not mean we only share our faith in our little part of the world, but that we are to find a way to fulfill the scope of His command.

We may look at the scale of a world-wide reach and become intimidated by its magnitude. However, if we are to be intentional in how we conduct our daily lives, we can be just as intentional in cooperative efforts to meet the diverse needs throughout the world while telling of the source of true freedom found in our Savior, Jesus Christ.

As citizens of a free nation we must be proactive in reaching out to other people groups for the propagation of freedom and God's message of love to all mankind. We risk losing the very freedoms we enjoy when we do not take full advantage to use those freedoms in exposing the world to both the advantages and benefits of it. Freedom must be held out like a beacon to the world, and credit for freedom's source must never be minimized or given a casual nod.

How different history may have been had Christians befriended Osama bin Laden while he was in America and exposed him to God's unconditional love. What a difference would have been made in the life of Adolf Hitler had those who taught him as a boy pointed to the words of a Savior Whose Kingdom would be a government represented by all nations. The relationship one has with The Creator is personal, but it was never meant to be private. How are you seeking to be the light of love to your community? What actions can be taken to connect hearts to the heart of God? True freedom penetrates God's truths throughout the world. **Will you pray for it? Pray with purpose for all cultures.**

"...make disciples

of all nations..."

Matthew 28:19 NIV

Going throughout the world demonstrating the benefits of a free society and a life liberated from the bondage of sin is a worthy endeavor. The work, though, does not stop there. The mandate Jesus gave His disciples was to **make disciples of all nations**: to make totally devoted followers of Christ, who will in turn, make other totally devoted followers of Christ, who will make.... You get the picture.

The first step of such an aggressive goal is leveraging the opportunity to connect with those docking on our shores, entering through our borders, or arriving at airports. Followers of Christ need to seize the opportunity to expose both legal and illegal visitors in our country to God's love and freedom's way.

George H.W. Bush once said, *"...we must not build walls of prejudice and doubt... We must build ties of mutual interests and affection everywhere."* (**Source:** Bush, George, *Heartbeat: George Bush in His Own Words*, p. 149.)   In fact, as citizens of Heaven we are commissioned to be transformed by the renewing of our minds and demonstrate such by how we love each other and treat our fellow man; thus transforming the world one life at a time. Making disciples is not accomplished in assembly-line fashion. It is a painstaking process of investing in another's life to point to our example and Lord, Jesus Christ.

Many Americans who remember September 11, 2001 are hesitant to seek the proliferation of freedom into countries hostile to our worldview. Our standard bearer prayed for forgiveness to those who brought Him such a cruel death. (Luke 23:34) Should we not also strive to bring our enemies into the light of forgiveness and love?

The question, then, is: are we willing to allow the Light of the world to use us in bringing Freedom's Life to *all* mankind?

O carrier of freedom's news, be swift-footed in your task in beginning foundations of freedom abroad. **Begin by praying for opportunities to connect with people groups near you.**

UNDERSTANDABLE
5
WORDS

"...my hope comes from Him."

Psalm 62: 5

Hope is generated by faith, for hope can only exist upon the platform of confidence in a reliable, firmly established person or pattern. God has placed patterns in His creation from the beginning: night and day, the phases of the moon, the processes of procreation, and the water cycle just to name a few. These dependable patterns foster our development of faith in Him, His Word, and His way. (Read Romans 1) The Bible teaches us that God is the source of faith and He will not disappoint. (Read Hebrews chapters 11-12)

The five simple words, *"my hope comes from Him"*, appear in a passage penned in the daily journal of David, a young shepherd who was elevated from the pasture to the prominent position of King. The prophet Samuel anointed David as the next king after Saul had refused to follow God's guidance. It was not until some fifteen years later that David began his rule over Judah, followed by the entire nation seven years later.

David was very familiar with waiting on God's timing. He discovered that the best cure for anxiety is hope, and David expressed his hope in God time and time again through the Psalms. It was his hope in Jehovah God, Who never sleeps (Psalm 121:4), that gave David the confidence of all things working together for his good. As David expressed his love and devotion to God, his life was blessed by God. (See Romans 8:28)

The Bible tells us that hope deferred makes the heart sick, but that hope fulfilled is like a tree of life. (Proverbs 13:12) In other words, hope fulfilled fuels more faith and confidence, which in turn fuels further hope in the source of that faith.

While in Capetown, South Africa, Robert F. Kennedy gave a well-crafted speech that hinted at Nelson Mandela's imprisonment. He described how hope works in the hearts and minds of others. In doing so, Kennedy was simply fueling the fire of hope in the hearts and minds of those who sought Mandela's release. Christian, understand the urgency of a time for righteousness to stand before America, demonstrating this same precept found in Kennedy's words:

"Each time a man stands up for an ideal or acts to improve the lot of others, or strikes out against injustice, he sends forth a tiny ripple of hope, and those ripples build a current which can sweep down the mightiest walls of oppression and resistance." (Robert F. Kennedy)
(Source: www.RFKcenter.org. Speech in Capetown, South Africa, June 6, 1966.)

It's true... hope was an integral part in the work of the Founders who risked their homes, livelihood, and life in their quest for independence. Without the hope of liberty in life's pursuit of happiness, all efforts toward such would be clouded with doubt. Renew hope for the human race, for our country: stand up for freedom's ideal and work to preserve it around the globe.

In praying for the proliferation of freedom around the world, pray that God will fuel hope in the hearts of patriots; and that this hope will, in turn, ignite courage to stand against atrocities of every kind.

"The hope of a Christian is inseparable from his faith. Whoever believes in the Divine inspiration of the Holy Scriptures must hope that the religion of Jesus shall prevail throughout the earth. Never since the foundation of the world have the prospects of mankind been more encouraging to that hope than they appear to be at the present time. And may the associated distribution of the Bible proceed and prosper till the Lord shall have made 'bare His holy arm in the eyes of all the nations, and all the ends of the earth shall see the salvation of our God'" [Isaiah 52:10].

John Quincy Adams

Sixth president of the United States; Secretary of State; U.S. Senator; U.S. Representative; Diplomat

Source: *Life of John Quincy Adams*, W. H. Seward, editor (Auburn, NY: Derby, Miller and Company, 1849), p. 248.

UNDERSTANDABLE
5
WORDS

"...my hope is in Thee."

Psalm 39:7

"...my hope is in Thee."

This prayer of five simple words is completely sufficient for the moment, not because God needs to hear it, but because we need to state our total dependence and confidence in Him and in His character to be our help and shield. (Psalm 91:2)

Hope provides nourishment to an otherwise impoverished heart. Hope motivates one to believe in the purpose of a stated end and invigorates one to persevere to that end. David had the conviction of such when he wrote:

> *"Why are you cast down,*
> *O my soul,*
> *and why are you in turmoil within?*
> *Hope in God;*
> *for I shall again praise Him,*
> *my salvation and my God."*
> (Psalm 42:5, KJV)

To a Christian, hope's perspective does not look through rose colored glasses. Instead, hope points the Believer to the Source of personal significance and the impact one's life will have for God's Kingdom. Paul put it this way:

> *"...Christ in you, the hope of glory!"*
> (Colossians 1:37)

It seems, then, that hope is circular: hope is fueled by faith; faith is generated and given by Jesus – in Whom we have placed our confidence; heaven is where Jesus reigns; God's glory is in heaven; heaven hopes the light of God's righteousness will shine through the life of every believer. That is why hope is a proprietor of freedom, an exporter of independence, an endorser of autonomy, for the world to see and know freedom's reality.

"...my hope is in Thee."

President Lyndon B. Johnson, when making his 1965 State of the Union address before Congress, ended his speech with:

> *"This then, is the state of the union:*
> *free and restless, growing and full of hope.*
> *So it was in the beginning.*
> *So it shall always be, while God is willing, and*
> *we are strong enough to keep the faith."* (January 5, 1965)

A free people we are, and a free people we shall remain, so long as we understand the source of that freedom and the hope fueled by it. **Pray with others across the nation that this hope will never perish from the earth. Put feet to your prayers by offering hope to those in desperate conditions or facing impossible odds.**

In God we trust.

This national motto, printed on the currency we use, was approved by an Act of the 84th Congress after recognizing it as foundational to the freedoms we enjoy. Its origin dates back to the War of 1812 when Francis Scott Key penned the words, *"and God is our trust"* as he wrote, *"The Star Spangled Banner"*.

Source: P.L. 84-140, US Government Publishing Office; www.gpo.gov

"I will hope in Him."

Job 13:15

There was a wealthy man named Job (pronounced, J-oh-b), who sought to live his life to be a blessing to his family and those who knew him. In the course of **one day** he experienced loss that would be difficult for anyone to endure:

> ➤ Enemies came into his land and took his property – his only means to make a living.
> ➤ Enemies also killed his employees and stole his fleet of pack animals needed for transporting goods in his business.
> ➤ All his children had been killed in a devastating natural disaster while gathered for a meal at the home of his oldest son.

Job's response to all that happened is recorded in the Bible within the section bearing his name:

> *"Naked I came from my mother's womb,*
> *and naked I shall return there.*
> *The Lord gave and the Lord has taken away.*
> *Blessed be the name of the Lord."*
> (Job 1:20-21)

In fact, the account goes on to say that through the entire episode Job did not sin or blame God. (v. 22) Not long thereafter Job became very ill with boils covering his entire body, causing great pain. His wife criticized him for his tenacious faith in God and told him to *"...curse God and die."* (Job 2:9)

Three friends heard of Job's adversity and came to comfort him. Upon seeing his condition, they were so struck with grief at seeing his pitiful state that no one spoke for seven days. Job began the conversation with a complaint against God. His friends reprimanded him for such. By the time he was able to speak again, he uttered today's five simple words from Job 13:15 which reflected the confidence Job had in God to turn it all around:

> *"Though He slay me,* ***I will hope in Him.***"

The story ends well for Job. Everything he lost was restored a hundred times more (Job 42:12), and he was also blessed with more children. He passed the test of hardship. He had peace within because he placed his hope in God and trusted in His love.

There have been times when we as a country have faced similar hardship. Almost every generation of Americans has experienced loss: wars, the Great Depression, prejudice, and social injustice; inequality in education, voting, and the workplace; hurricanes, tornadoes, earthquakes, fires, floods, and mudslides have all been recorded in the history of our great country.

Each generation has been able to hear the clarion call of peace in the midst of the turmoil... *until recently.* It seems our nation has lost sight of hope's source... freedom's fuel. The nation of America in 2015 is suffering from a severe deficiency of peace. What are some of the symptoms? Well, other than what is obvious in the daily news, how about the following?

> ➢ The failure of marriage, thus the breakdown of the American home and liberal attacks on the traditional model.
> ➢ The uncertainty of investments, creating a population of greed mongers who seek to rob others of savings that may have taken a lifetime to build. Do the names Enron and Bernie Madoff sound familiar?
> ➢ The nation-wide decline in church attendance.

What is the solution or cure to these trends? A tenacious audacious faith in the One Who guided the founding of this nation, Jesus Christ, by those believers who will not shrink back in articulating those precepts of faith for the next generation. Hope in Him as the Savior, not only of our souls, but of our nation and our world. **Pray for those who will not shrink in the face of opposition, that they will have courage to stand while also reflecting the peace and love of Christ.**

"No candid observer will deny that whatever of good there may be in our American civilization is the product of Christianity. Still less can he deny that the grand motives which are working for the elevation and purification of our society are strictly Christian... A belief in Jesus Christ is the very fountainhead of everything that is desirable and praise worthy in our civilization, and this civilization is the flower of time."

Theodore Roosevelt

Source: Roosevelt, Theodore, *Springfield Republican,* 1884, editorial.

UNDERSTANDABLE 5 WORDS

"...having been justified

by faith..."

Romans 5:1

Paul is exposing the young church in Rome to distinguish between legalism and grace. It seems that the early Christians were confused on the utility of the law in revealing the idea of sin. The meaning of today's five simple words is found as early as the third chapter:

> *"But now the **righteousness** of God*
> *has been manifested*
> *apart from the law,*
> *although the law and the prophets*
> *bear witness to it –*
> *the righteousness of God*
> *through faith in Jesus Christ*
> *for all who believe.*
> *For there is no distinction:*
> *for all have sinned and fall short of*
> *the glory of God,*
> *and are justified by His grace as a gift,*
> *through the redemption that is in Christ Jesus,*
> *Whom God put forward as a*
> *propitiation by His blood,*
> *to be received by faith."*
> (Romans 3:21-25, ESV)

Paul directed them back to their historical roots, and reminded them of Abraham and how he was justified by His faith, not works. He comes to the first of several powerful concluding remarks when he states:

> *"Therefore, **having been justified by faith**,*
> *we have peace with God*
> *through our Lord Jesus Christ."*
> (Romans 5:1; bold added for emphasis)

Once peace with God is secured in one's life, that same peace works within the believer to reveal the God of peace to others. How many lives lost to suicide could have been rescued through this peace? How many marriages could have survived because of this peace? What hasty decisions could have been thwarted by the security of such peace? How many wars could have been averted because of this peace?

"...having been justified by faith..."

A nation that embraces and exports freedom must be a people *justified by faith* that blesses the nations with the olive branch of God's peace. The proliferation of freedom brings with it the commitment to negotiate peace, for with peace comes an ally, expanding commerce, and an open door for the truth of God's Word to penetrate more people groups so they, too, may know freedom's benefits.

> *"Blessed are the peacemakers,*
> *for they shall be called sons of God."*
> (Matthew 5:9)

Justification by faith is part of the foundation for a free society. When a nation's citizens experience such peace, the relationships in marriage, family, business, politics, and worship are preserved and nourished as they thrive in an environment of peace. Peace, to you and your household.

Approach God's throne boldly, knowing this justification has granted you complete access to Him. Leverage the opportunities each day brings to spread this founding precept of freedom's origin by articulating to those whose lives you intersect. Ask God to prepare the hearts and minds of those who will receive these eternal benefits.

"...stand firm in the faith..."

1 Corinthians 6:1

Peace is not a weak virtue. Peace stands upon the strength by which it is achieved. Paul was encouraging the Corinthians to *stand firm in the faith* – which was also *their* faith, since coming to live in the light of God's grace. He instructed them to act like men, not to be weak, but to show peace through strength... the strength of love. This is the lever Jesus instructed all men to use in the exercise of reaching the hardened hearts of mankind.

So, how are we to *stand firm in the faith*? When writing to the church in Ephesus, Paul gave the prerequisites for such:

> *"Put on the full armor of God, so that you will be able to stand firm against the schemes of the devil."*
> (Ephesians 6:11)

That full armor consisted of:

- ➢ The breastplate of righteousness.
- ➢ Footwear for spreading God's good news of peace.
- ➢ The shield of faith.
- ➢ The helmet of salvation.
- ➢ The sword of the Spirit, which is God's Word.

Did you notice that there was no part of the armor covering the backside? Cowardice in the face of opposition isn't expected. The true soldier of light will guard the heart (Proverbs 4:23) against prejudice, envy, lust, and all forms of corruption. Paul also advised that patriots taking on this third dimension of battle should pray at all times and watch out for fellow Believers.

The protector of all that is good and right will leverage every open door to share the good news of peace through Jesus Christ. The warrior of light will never forsake allegiance to the Author of Freedom, and will grow in the understanding of God's Word. The Freedom Fighter will use that familiarity of the Word to attack the strongholds of darkness with eternal truths, and will stay in constant communication with The Commander of the heavenly hosts to receive the marching orders for the battle that will require proficiency with the Sword of the Spirit.

Heaven's combatants will be on the alert for potential threats, and will look after each other, taking every effort to see to each other's needs. The unseen battle is often the critical exchange that will give the advantage on the world's battlefields. Let freedom's ring courageously display truth and righteousness as we stand firm upon Heaven's eternal truths, the truths which the Founders of this nation recognized as freedom's origin.

"It is most evident that this land is under the protection of the Almighty, and that we shall be saved not by our wisdom nor by our might, but by the Lord of Host Who is wonderful in counsel and Almighty in all His operations."

Oliver Wolcott

SIGNER OF THE DECLARATION OF INDEPENDENCE; MILITARY GENERAL; GOVERNOR OF CONNECTICUT

Source: *Letters of Delegates to Congress: January 1, 1776-May 15, 1776*, Paul H. Smith, editor (Washington DC: Library of Congress, 1978), Vol. 3, pp. 502-503, Oliver Wolcott to Laura Wolcott on April 10, 1776.

Pray that leaders of the free world will be fully equipped to face the schemes devised against them, and to *stand firm in the faith* through righteous living.

Oliver Wolcott

DECLARATION OF INDEPENDENCE
CONNECTICUT

UNDERSTANDABLE
5
WORDS

*"The Lord preserves
the faithful..."*

Psalm 31:23

Just how *the Lord preserves the faithful* may be up for debate. In fact, David begins this psalm by declaring his trust and dependence on God to protect and care for him. Then he writes of the incredible stress he is under because of past sins, the constant threat of attack by enemies, his embarrassment by the scorn of his neighbors and by the revealed plans of those who seek to assassinate him. He states that he is a *"broken vessel"*. (Psalm 31: 12)

David does, however, restate his complete confidence in God to protect, guide, confirm, and establish his life. David beams with confidence in God's favor toward those He loves with the words:

"How great is Your goodness which You have stored up for those who fear You... You hide them in the secret place of Your presence from the conspiracies of man." (Psalm 31:19-20)

Today, conspiracies abound on all fronts, targeted attacks meant to weaken and dismantle free societies. Citizens of free nations must be vigilant to protect their countries from assaults – foreign or domestic, as sometimes the enemy is found to be within the chambers of those in positions of influence to the leaders of the free world.

It is refreshing to see how David expressed his dependence and confidence in the Author of Freedom, Who preserved his heritage and legacy to this very day as evidenced in The Bible. God will do the same for leaders today who will follow David's example.

The second verse to the hymn, *"How Firm a Foundation"*, describes God's faithfulness in preserving those bearing His name:

"Fear not I am with thee,
O be not dismayed,
For I am thy God
and will still give thee aid;
I'll strengthen thee, help thee,
And cause thee to stand,
Upheld by My gracious omnipotent hand."

May God preserve our country, our freedoms, and our faith! The Founders relied upon this precept, risking their family, property, and work in their pursuit of liberty. **Pray with me that God will preserve this country and will raise up leaders like David who will stand upon the foundation of faith in God, the same foundation upon which our founding fathers placed their confidence. Pray for those in emergency services, police and fire personnel, and those receiving the emergency calls at 911 centers across our country – all of these who are so reliable in their work. Thank God for their faithfulness. Ask for God to move through the emergency services community to drawing hearts to His Kingdom.**

"...the safety and prosperity of nations ultimately and essentially depend on the protection and blessing of Almighty God; and the national acknowledgment of this truth is not only an indispensable duty which the people owe to Him, but a duty whose natural influence is favorable to the promotion of that morality and piety, without which social happiness cannot exist, nor the blessings of a free government be enjoyed..."

John Adams

Recorded and submitted by Timothy Pickering, Secretary of State on March 23, 1798

Source: Proclamation reprinted in the Columbian Centinal, April 4, 1798.

UNDERSTANDABLE 5 WORDS

"…that you may have life…"

John 5:39

In this passage, Jesus describes Himself as the gate or the way to God's Kingdom and abundant life. The life Jesus described is not a mere existence to endure, but a life to be lived, cherished, enjoyed, and valued. Once a life has experienced freedom it can be expressed through: successful enterprise, protection of the home, sacred worship, and inclusion to one's community. Our founding fathers stated:

> *"We hold these truths to be self-evident,*
> *that all men are created equal,*
> *that they are endowed by their Creator*
> *with certain unalienable Rights,*
> *that among these are*
> *Life, Liberty and the pursuit of Happiness."*
> (**Source**: *The Declaration of Independence*, paragraph 2)

To those who are free, life without the value of quality is no life at all. Our forefathers developed a list of grievances sent to the King of England which included: interference in establishing local laws; dissolving representative forms of governance; disallowing trial by jury; maintaining an active army in the colonies, an army that could demand quartering without compensation; that same army subverting existing laws; and taxation without representation. (**Source**: *The Declaration of Independence*)

The list of grievances developed by these patriots did not develop overnight. As the offenses by England grew, the British Army eventually grew to dominate the colonies. In the same way, sin can creep into our life pattern and eventually overtake our ability to master the domain of our hearts and minds. We either master life or life master's us.

Abundant living occurs when we discover the value of giving our life away for God's Kingdom. It takes personal sacrifice and the commitment to insure freedom for all, not just oneself.

Jesus' death on the cross was given for all who will come to Him in faith for freedom from sin's curse and that we may, *"live as free men, yet without using... freedom as a pretext for evil; but... as servants of God."* (I Peter 2:16)

From Him springs the core of *freedom's foundation*. Paul explained it to the Ephesians this way:

> *"...you are fellow citizens with the saints, and are of God's household, having been built on the foundation of the apostles and prophets, Christ Jesus Himself being the corner stone."* (Ephesians 2:19-20)

Some measure life in time, others by their life experience, still others by their legacy. However any one of us may measure life, this life is not a permanent state; it will come to an end. As long as we have the rights to *life, liberty, and the pursuit of happiness*, let us live in a way that preserves those same rights for the next generation, thereby establishing a very real legacy of freedom with a foundation that will last for generations to come.

As you pray for this free nation, pray for freedom to be granted to following generations. Pray for families to know abundant life in their pursuits of happiness as they are exposed to the Source of Peace.

UNDERSTANDABLE 5 WORDS

"…you are… a holy nation"

I Peter 2:9

113

Since the beginning of the new free nation Moses led to the Promised Land, the influence of holiness has been a part of God's purpose for those He claims. In fact, Peter's inspiration for this passage came directly from Levitical law:

"Thus you are to be holy..., for I the Lord am holy; and I have set you apart from the peoples to be Mine." (Leviticus 20:26)

The word, *"holy"*, in Hebrew is 'qa-dosh', and carries with it the meaning of consecrated or set apart for a significant righteous purpose. Let that sink in. As followers of Christ, we are set apart for God's righteous (*fair and accurate*) purposes. We become, in essence, envoys of heaven... ambassadors on a royal mission... each commissioned by the King of Kings. (Read Matthew 28:19-20) This leads to a worldview that nothing is left to circumstance in the life of the Believer. I love the way the paraphrased *Living Bible* expresses the following passages:

"...the Lord directs the steps of the Godly,
He delights in every detail of their lives."
(Psalm 37:23; LB)

"We can make our plans,
but the Lord determines our steps."
(Proverbs 16:9)

Peter described the purpose for which we are set apart; the essential work we have been created to accomplish. He further distinguishes those who follow Christ by four qualifying descriptions:

"But you are a chosen race,
a royal priesthood,
a holy nation,
a people for God's Own possession,
so that you may proclaim
the excellencies of Him
Who has called you out of darkness
into His marvelous light."
(I Peter 2:9)

"...you are... a holy nation..."

The phrase, *"a chosen race"*, may come across as negative to some. However, Peter is not speaking in exclusive terms. He is describing the adoption God exercises when He rescues lost souls from the grip of darkness. The new Believer becomes, as Jesus put it, *"born again"*. (Read John 3:1-21) Thus the chosen race is a nationality that is not of this world. (Read John 18:36)

Peter then describes Christ followers as a *"royal priesthood"*. This, too, reflects back to the Mosaic law describing the nation of Israel:

> *"and you shall be to Me a kingdom of priests*
> *and a holy nation."*
> (Exodus 19:6)

The priests interceded for the nation in the prayers offered to God. It was God's system of demonstrating His desire to keep the connection between Israel and Himself.

The words *"holy nation"* in Greek can be accurately translated as a peculiar ethnic group or race as we understand it today. Again, it was not written in a way that was derogatory to other people groups. In fact, it was used to show the first century church that just as they could tell a Jew from a Gentile, so the lives of Believers should be just as apparent a difference to the world by their love and lifestyle.

Peter was inspired to elaborate further, calling Christians, *"a people for God's own possession"*. There was to be no doubt, in the world's eyes, the ability to identify Christ followers. The purpose Peter gave for those who had been set apart was so simple a child could understand it – to tell others about God's rich mercy and how He delivers from the oppression of darkness for the freedom of His eternal light.

The descriptions Peter used for any new Believer provided the significance of their identity with Christ, empowering them to persevere under great persecution.

The richness of this one passage declares God's unlimited grace to all who will believe, as well as the power of His light to illumine the entire world toward a government of righteousness and peace. The Founders knew that the dynamics of this government would expose the faults of slavery, corruption, prejudice, etc., all common to mankind, and that such besetting vices would be neutralized through God's transforming power. Though it has taken more than three hundred years, the power of God's truths are effectually exposing and eliminating those obstacles of freedom.

When praying for one's nation, spiritual petitions should not be withheld for truth to expose corruption in high places as it scatters the darkness of deception. Pray that righteousness will, indeed, exalt this nation as a holy nation admired by the world.

"For a child will be born to us,
a son will be given to us;
and the government will
rest on His shoulders;
and His name will be called:
Wonderful, Counselor,
Mighty God, Eternal Father,
Prince of Peace.
There will be no end to
the increase of His government
or of peace...
the zeal of the Lord of hosts
will accomplish this."
Isaiah 9:6-7

"…be hospitable to

one another…"

1 Peter 4:9

Webster's dictionary defines hospitality as the *"generous and friendly treatment of visitors and guests"*. I grew up in the South where the practice is widened to neighbors, newcomers, and the surrounding community. The golden rule of treating others the way one would like to be treated is deeply imbedded in Southern culture, and is really what Peter is described when he wrote to the first century church.

There were many barriers to be overcome by those first Believers. The barriers of status and achievement were overcome as people were attracted to the Light of the world and the change it brought to their lives. Change that brought ridicule by their former associates. (I Peter 4:4)

In today's *five understandable words*, Peter had just reminded the reader that love covers a multitude of sins and to be firmly devoted in love to all who come to Christ. He instructed them to be hospitable, and then he added a qualifier: *"without complaint"*. Peter guided them to let their hospitality be genuine, not just some outward show to impress others.

When we are hospitable *"without complaint"*, we are willing to either overlook or make the special effort toward those who are demanding, prejudiced, difficult, or even ornery. (I give such people the description of EGR: Extra Grace Required!) Biblical hospitality follows the pattern of Christ, Who took on the role of a servant… even to the point of washing His disciples' feet.

What does this type of hospitality have to do with freedom? It is the embodiment of a truly free people offering freedom to those exiled from their homelands and is beautifully described in a poem that was read at the opening ceremonies to the Statue of Liberty (a plaque of the poem was installed in 1903):

> *"Give me your tired, your poor,*
> *Your huddled masses yearning to breathe free,*
> *The wretched refuse of your teeming shore.*
> *Send these, the homeless tempest-tost to me,*
> *I lift my lamp beside the golden door!"*
> (By Emma Lazarus, 1849-1887)

118

Let our hospitality ring the invitation of sanctuary for the exiled! This foundation of freedom is never exclusive. **Pray for the courage to: seek understanding of others; connect to the disenfranchised; assist the needy and provide shelter for the homeless; and work that all your efforts toward such would honor and glorify the One Who did not turn us away. It can be summarized in the *five understandable words* below:**

"Love thy neighbor as thyself."

Mark 12:31 (KJV)

UNDERSTANDABLE **5** WORDS

"…seek peace and pursue it…"

Psalm 34:14

Though freedom comes at the great cost measured by the blood given in both acquiring and protecting it, freedom always seeks peace. It is during peacetime that the garden of happiness can be tended by the hands of wisdom and perseverance. It is in peace that we are able to pursue life, liberty, and happiness. It is during a nation's chapter of peace that its citizens are able to take full advantage in pursuing the vision for the life one desires - fulfilling the potential for which God created each person. The season of peace provides one the full liberty to be focused on such endeavors without being burdened and bound by the constraints of warfare, though, national security will always be the responsibility of every conscientious citizen.

In today's *five understandable words* we observe that King David crafted the text carefully. This counsel was given to his heirs and his countrymen. It is not enough just to *seek* peace, for many times it will be met with resistance. Patriots cannot justify contentions or conflicts without first *pursuing* every available means for achieving peace.

Such was the case with our founding fathers who sought peace with England's tyrannical king. *The Declaration of Independence* was developed only after many efforts toward peace. The colonists first sought to appeal to the sanity of negotiation through ten years of legislative acts that were each dismissed or rejected by England. In fact, the colonists were treated more harshly with each effort toward reconciliation.

In 1776, the patriot, Thomas Paine anonymously published the pamphlet, *"Common Sense"*, which galvanized the colonies into taking action toward independence. In *"Common Sense"* Paine stated the arguments against British rule that included taxation without representation, oppressive rule by a foreign army, and England ignoring attempts by the colonists to establish a local judiciary. In the third edition, Paine added clarification to his arguments and gave these concluding remarks:

"We have it in our power to begin the world over again. A situation, similar to the present, hath not happened since the days of Noah until now." (**Source:** Paine, Thomas, *Common Sense.* 3rd edition, 1776)

The Founders' motivations were Biblical in both scope and quality. The framers earnestly desired to form a nation under the ideals of scripture: to be *"free indeed"*. (Read John 8:31-36) They asserted that the peace of God can only be known and lived by those who know the God of peace, Who revealed Himself through the Prince of Peace. (Read Philippians 4:4-9; Isaiah 9:6-7)

It is in finding the freedom He gives that leads us to strive for the freedoms by which we live. Other worldviews are juxtaposed to this way of thinking. President John Quincy Adams provided some clarifying thoughts on opposing worldviews:

> *[The] "...law of nations as practiced among Christian nations . . .
> is founded upon the principle that the state of nature
> between men and between nations is a state of peace.
> But there was a Mohometan law of nations
> which considered the state of nature as a state of war."*
> **John Quincy Adams**
> (**Source**: John Quincy Adams, *The Jubilee of the Constitution*, 1839, p. 73.)

We are experiencing a very similar contest of cultures today. Almost daily we are confronted with the worldviews of liberalism, atheism, and sharia law, etc., and the extreme measures of those embracing these worldviews.

Those who know God's peace are willing to give their lives for others to gain a life of liberty. Jesus promised the power of His peace to every follower who would take up his/her cross and follow Him:

> *"Peace I leave with you; My peace I give to you; not as the world gives do I give to you. Do not let your heart be troubled, nor let it be fearful."* (John 14:27)

As we ***seek peace and pursue it*** by relating to other nations and cultures, we extend the olive branch of peace found in Christ and trust the Holy Spirit to do His supernatural work.

As immigrants to America arrive on our shores, we have a wonderful opportunity to make a compelling case for peace through Christ, in the abundant life He offers, as our Cornerstone for the liberties we enjoy, and the platform upon which we seek to coexist. In doing so, we provide a rich resource which we can use to export the ideals of Christianity and its basis for a free society to nations around the world. How? The internationals within our borders, after hearing the ideals spoken by our mouths and after seeing those ideals lived out through our lives, will tell of such to their friends and loved ones abroad.

One example of this is found in the report on the growing Christian population given by Aristedes to Emporer Hadrian:

"...if one or other of them have bondmen and bondwomen or children, through love towards them they persuade them to become Christians, and when they have done so, they call them brethren without distinction... They don't consider themselves brothers in the usual sense, but brothers instead through the spirit, in God."
(**Source:** Kirby, Peter, *"Historical Jesus Theories"*, *Early Christian Writings*. 2015)

Foundational to any free society is peace between nations and cultures. It cannot be given lip service only; we must pursue it diligently. May God grant us peace in our time. **The lip service we do give to it should be by intercession for peace between nations and cultures. Will you pray for peace on our streets, in our cities and towns, between cultures, and around the world?**

"*...greater love hath no man...*"

John 15:13 (KJV)

Jesus is preparing the disciples for the time of His departure. He had already described heaven to them and how he was preparing a place for them (and for us who bear His name). Then these five simple words seem to come out of nowhere: ***"greater love hath no man"***. (John 15:13)

He goes on to say that when they are hated by the world to remember that He was hated by the world before they experienced such. (John 15:18) Righteous love, like liberty, is despised and rejected by the world. When Pilate, the Roman governor over Israel, presided at the trial of Jesus, he found no fault with him and offered to the crowd a choice: the thief and murderer, Barabbas (Read Acts 3:14), or Jesus. The crowd chose Barabbas. (Read Luke 23)

Righteous liberty will be despised in the same way. People who have never experienced the joy of freedom are blinded to its benefits and blessings. Our founding fathers resolved to confront the mightiest army and navy of their day for the risk of a life in pursuit of happiness, free from despotism. This should remind each American of a heritage we are all called on to protect.

Jesus did not paint a very pretty picture when describing the world's treatment to those who would follow Him:

> *"You will be hated by all*
> *because of My name,*
> *but it is the one*
> *who has endured to the end*
> *who will be saved."*
> (Matthew 10:22)

Perhaps our enemies are not only motivated to destroy our freedoms, but the source of our liberty.

The entire statement made by Jesus in today's *five understandable words* described the dynamics of this love: *"...**greater love hath no man** than this, that one lay down his life for his friends."* (John 15:13) Jesus was pointing to his impending death on a cross. However, both His words and His death point to the premise of freedom's price.

126

"...greater love hath no man..."

The cost of freedom has always been measured in blood: beginning from the blood that flowed from Calvary's hill, to that spilled by those who fought against tyranny, to those who defend the cause of independence today.

Stories abound about those who faced incredible odds during conflicts. I have been moved by the stories of Joe Foss, Clebe McClary, and Jackie Bayne, men I have known or met. Even my own father's heroism was recently celebrated in Fanano, Italy, where he had been shot down during his military service in World War 2. He evaded capture by the Germans for an entire week, aided by Italian nationals assisting him back to allied soil. (November, 1944; MACR 9981) There are new stories being written from the battlefields of the Middle-East, along our coastline and borders, across the world or across a city street in America that reveal new heroes in the battle for freedom's cause.

Freedom is sacred – just as described in the hymn, *"America the Beautiful"*:

> *"O beautiful for heroes proved*
> *In liberating strife,*
> *Who more than self their country loved*
> *And mercy more than life!"*

Foundational to all freedom is its cost. It's been said that freedom may be free but it certainly isn't cheap.

Pray for our military and their families that deal with a host of issues as they stand in harm's way: separation during assignments; PTSD; amputees; transition to civilian life; etc. Pray for emergency, police and fire personnel who face complex and stressful situations daily. Give thanks for their service to protect freedom and perpetuate freedom's cause. Ask God to bless these precious families with His favor, care, and protection.

128

UNDERSTANDABLE 5 WORDS

"...able men who fear God..."

Exodus 18:21

As the nation of Israel wandered in the desert, there came a time when their leader Moses was stuck in the quagmire of the daily issues of this new nation. It was such an obvious distraction to Moses' father-in-law, Jethro, that he counseled Moses on the issue:

"'What is this thing that you are doing for the people? Why do you alone sit as judge and all the people stand about you from morning until evening?' Moses said to his father-in-law, 'Because the people come to me to inquire of God. When they have a dispute, it comes to me, and I judge between a man and his neighbor and make known the statutes of God and His laws.'"

*"Moses' father-in-law said to him, 'The thing that you are doing is not good. You will surely wear out, both yourself and these people who are with you, for the task is too heavy for you; you cannot do it alone. Now listen to me: I will give you counsel and God be with you. You be the people's representative before God, and you bring the disputes to God, then teach them the statutes and the laws, and make known to them the way in which they are to walk and the work they are to do. Furthermore, you shall select out of all the people **able men who fear God**, men of truth, those who hate dishonest gain; and you shall place these over them as leaders of thousands, of hundreds, of fifties, and of tens. Let them judge the people at all times; and let it be that every major dispute they will bring to you, but every minor dispute, they themselves will judge. So it will be easier for you, and they will bear the burden with you. If you do this thing and God so commands you, then you will be able to endure, and all these people also will go to their place in peace.'"* (Exodus 18:14-23)

Moses heeded the advice of Jethro and thus began the development toward civil elected government for a free society. Jethro wanted Moses to get it right and provided qualifying descriptions for these judicial representatives of the people: *"men of truth who hate dishonest gain."* This was foundational to the efficient workings of the new republic and remains essential for elected officials today.

Citizens who take their role seriously will measure the worth of those running for office by these two simple qualifications. Those who embrace the value of truth provide the stumbling block to those who devise lies in circumventing the ways of righteousness.

Those who loath dishonest gains act as society's filter to charlatans who prey on the ignorance of uninformed people, and to hucksters who slyly craft dishonest words to look as wholesome as apple pie. Representatives who are passionately opposed to those who play cat and mouse with the truth are to act as guardians in the sacred halls of freedom.

I love the name, *"Able"*. In Hebrew, the name could have two meanings; both are appropriate, considering Abel's brief life. Abel's first meaning is *"vapor"*, implying the shortness of life. The second meaning for "Abel" is *"mourning"*. The use of either is appropriate when describing the life of one who was murdered by his own brother. So, how does this word affect the phrase we ponder today?

Though etymologists date the word, "able", back to a fourteenth century French derivation of the Latin word, *"habilis"*, meaning easily handled. It is the name, *"Abel"*, which makes a more fitting description of representatives who fear God. The significance of the word rests poignantly upon the description of the office of a representative.

Representatives in our Congress are those who serve for two years, a period that can seem as brief as a *vapor*. (Read James 4:13-17) If they take their role seriously they will redeem the little time they have to make a difference. (Read Ephesians 5:6-16) Those who endeavor to walk soberly know the power of darkness that seeks to overthrow the strengths found in Liberty's values, giving pause to *mourn* the sad condition of those whose minds have been polluted by corruption and vice of every kind.

"Abel" people who fear God provides a foundational perspective granted through the Founders. **Use your vote wisely and pray for *"Abel"* leaders who will display the foundational characteristic of righteousness in their living and thinking.**

"Governments... depend upon men than men upon governments... Let men be good and the government cannot be bad... though good laws do well, good men do better; for good laws may want (lack) good men... but good men will never want (lack) good laws nor suffer (allow bad) ill ones." **William Penn**

Source: Clarkson, Thomas, *Memoirs of the Private and Public Life of William Penn*, Vol. I, p. 303.

"They must also be acquainted with the rules of righteousness; they must know what is just and what is unjust, be 'able men,'...."

Source: Samuel Willard, 1640-1707, Quoting from the Library of American Literature by Stedman and Hutchinson, 1889.

UNDERSTANDABLE **5** WORDS

"when... righteous rule...

people rejoice..."

Proverbs 29:2

In this poignant proverb Solomon makes a simple contrast that expresses the heart of a free people and that of an oppressed people. When people are governed by *fair and accurate* laws with leaders who cherish and submit themselves to the same, the people of that nation will be glad. In fact, they will celebrate the goodness and liberty found through them.

Conversely, when wicked people subvert the cause of righteousness and become the rulers of the day, the people groan. (Proverbs 29:2) It becomes painfully obvious that their freedoms have been infringed upon; their liberties have been overly regulated; their property and possessions overly-taxed; and their pursuit of happiness quenched under exclusive regimes who define the 'haves' and the 'have-nots'.

When the righteous rule, there will be opportunity to achieve; a prospect to prosper; and the advantage to attain more knowledge, more wealth, and a greater vision to succeed. When the righteous legislate, there are celebrations lauding the integrity of devout, faithful men and women who seek to live out the precepts of freedom found in the handbook to happiness, and who seek to better their communities and nation.

When the righteous govern, even the lives of the poor are improved by the increased wealth of charitable minds. National efforts are enhanced for efficient ways to provide for the impoverished when people of integrity lead. Public safety officers are more highly respected and honored when enforcement is meant to guide those whose minds think on the things of God:

"...whatever is true... honorable... right... pure... lovely... whatever is of good repute, if there is any excellence and if anything worthy of praise, dwell on these..." (Philippians 4:8)

An honorable leader is a gift to a nation from a righteous God Who reigns in the affairs of mankind. With God there are no coincidences. A good example of how God reigns in the affairs of nations is found in the life of Daniel.

During the time of Israel's captivity, the ruling king had a troubling dream that none of his counselors could interpret. So, the king gave the order to have all the counselors slain. A young Jewish man, Daniel, was a part of that group of counselors. Daniel asked his friends to pray for God to show him the meaning of the king's dream, as his very life depended on it... literally! The mystery of the dream was revealed to Daniel in a night vision. That revelation was summed up in the words of Daniel's worship to God before entering the king's presence:

"Let the name of God
be blessed forever and ever,
for wisdom and power belong to Him.
It is He Who changes the times
and the epochs;
He removes kings and establishes kings;
He gives wisdom to wise men
and knowledge to men of understanding."
(Daniel 2:20-21)

Daniel delivered the interpretation of the dream to the Persian king who actually honored Daniel with great tribute by electing him ruler of the province as well as chief of all the king's advisors. Daniel's revelation further confirms God's mighty hand in the affairs of nations. In his parting address to Congress, President George Washington affirmed the value of our nation's righteous origins:

"Of all the dispositions and habits which lead to political prosperity, religion and morality are indispensable supports." Washington further stated, *"Whatever may be conceded to the influence of refined education on men of peculiar structure, reason, and experience both forbid us to expect that national morality can prevail in exclusion of religious principle."* (**Source:** 1796 Farewell Address marking Washington's exit from his duties as President and Commanding Officer.)

Pray that free nations around the world will have reasons to rejoice in righteous leaders who have been prepared through God's providential hand. Pray for our country to have such a leader.

"By renouncing the Bible, philosophers swing from their moorings upon all moral subjects... It is the only correct map of the human heart that ever has been published..."

Benjamin Rush

Source: Benjamin Rush, *Letters of Benjamin Rush*, January 23, 1807.

UNDERSTANDABLE **5** WORDS

"...a disgrace to any people..."

Proverbs 14:34

In keeping with the definition of righteousness given at the first of the book, the virtues of **accuracy** and *fairness* will make a nation stand out among the rest. Just how is this so?

Accuracy deals with truth: truth in one's work, truth in one's relationships, truth in one's perspective or worldview. If our worldview is not accurate with reality, it distorts our perception of everything and everyone else around us. A distorted worldview leads to: shallow relationships; deceptive work practices; and a personal allegiance to falsehood. These distorted values result in: a detachment from society; delinquency in one's work; and despair in the midst of failure.

The United States is still a young nation. It has always wrestled with her identity as *"one nation under God"*. Though the country as we know it began as a refuge for those seeking freedom of speech and the practice of their faith, there were many who landed on the shores of freedom not sharing the same worldview.

Just as there were patriots who loved God's way and fought for independence, there were also those who fought for independence for many other reasons. From the beginning, a hidden war has waged in our land to distract its citizens of the purposes of righteousness and deter any advancement of heaven's Kingdom. Paul described this covert conflict:

> *"For we wrestle not against flesh and blood,*
> *but against principalities, against powers,*
> *against the rulers of the darkness of this world,*
> *against spiritual wickedness in high places."*
> (Ephesians 6:12, KJV)

Though unseen by earthly eyes, it is nevertheless a very real battle. It is a strategic battle which is why we must always be ready for the conflict; always wearing the full armor of God. (Read Ephesians 6:10-18) We must always be aware that darkness is on the move. (Read 1 Peter 5:8)

But we need not be dismayed, for the Prince of Peace has equipped us for such a time as this:

> *"For though we live in the world,*
> *we do not wage war as the world does.*
> *The weapons we fight with are not*
> *the weapons of the world.*
> *On the contrary, they have divine power*
> *to demolish strongholds.*
>
> *We demolish arguments and*
> *every pretension that sets itself up*
> *against the knowledge of God,*
> *and we take captive every thought*
> *to make it obedient to Christ."*
> (2 Corinthians 10:3-5)

So, you see, we are engaged in a conflict over the hearts and minds of men, women, and children assaulted by unrighteous ideas, evidenced by The United States as the largest exporter of pornography in the world. We live in a time of human trafficking, the threat of terrorism, random 'drive-by' shootings, anarchy on our city streets, in-school shootings, drug abuse, abortion on demand, corruption in business and government, increasing social detachment and many other social ills which have proliferated our society. Political correctness has only produced cowards of those who profess to hold freedom's light, further corrupting any influence for good.

Foundational in the maintenance of a free society is a citizenry whose lives are marked by integrity, duty, mercy, faith, and love. These are the virtues that will elevate a nation's status and position in the world. Owning-up to the faults and failures of one's past is essential to integrity. King David exhibited such in his prayer for forgiveness. He was acutely aware of the wrongs he had committed and sought out God's path for restoration. It is recorded in Psalm 51. He knew that *righteousness exalts a nation and that sin is a reproach to any people.* A higher calling leads to a higher walk. **Will you take that higher walk in prayer?** Perhaps the following prayer will assist your intercession for America today.

"Supremely great and infinitely glorious Lord our God! From everlasting to everlasting Thou art the same! Unchangeable in Thy works! Clothed with light as with a garment, and with majesty as with a robe! Who maketh the clouds Thy chariot, and walkest upon the wings of the winds! Possessed of every adorable ATTRIBUTE and divine PERFECTION!

We, Thy unworthy but dependent children, assembled on this joyful occasion, humbly desire to approach the THRONE of Thy GRACE, in and through the merit of Thy coequal SON, our EVER BLESSED SAVIOR! For HIS sake, be pleased to pardon our manifold sins, and to blot out all our transgressions!! Justify our persons through Immanuel's righteousness, and sanctify our natures by the powerful influences of Thy most holy Spirit! May we wholly be devoted to Thy service, and live uniformly to Thy praise!"

Source: The Massachusetts Centinal, Wednesday, August 15, 1787. A portion of the prayer offered by Rev. William Rogers; July 4, at the Reformed Calvinist Church, Philadelphia, PA, that same year.

UNDERSTANDABLE 5 WORDS

"...I will... judge the nation..."

Genesis 15:14

"...I will... judge the nation..."

Accountability... it's a precept that began in the Garden of Eden. From the very beginning God informed mankind that there are consequences for one's actions... even for nations. The passage containing these five powerful words, spoken by God to Abraham, describes how God will fulfill His promise to Abraham and make a great nation of his progeny, a people that would be taken captive and, after many years, be rescued to inhabit the Promised Land.

God stated that there would be consequences for an entire nation. Take a moment to consider this thought... it's sobering to think that the creator of the universe has standards by which He judges nations; standards that He takes very seriously.

Many national leaders, including our own, have given a respectful nod of recognition to the Eternal Throne of Righteousness while conducting the affairs of the nation in appalling and undisciplined ways. It rings true to the ear that absolute power corrupts absolutely, especially when we are already corrupted by our own wantonness. Leaders of nations have an awesome responsibility which should never be taken lightly. Foundational to that responsibility is to lead in righteousness and truth. Such leadership is transparent and forthright; a value missing in many leaders today.

Even the most respected leaders of the modern era have displayed poor decisions in personal and sometimes national environs. Thumbing one's nose at the righteous precepts of God does not bode well for a leader or a nation. The nation God was referring to in today's passage was Egypt... and the judgment was severe:

➢ Water was turned to blood, killing all the fish and making the water unfit to drink and limiting their existing food supply. (Exodus 7:14-25)
➢ Frogs infested the land, defiling the beds and the kitchens in both the freeman and slaves homes. (Exodus 7:26 – 8:11)
➢ Gnats or lice as numerous as the Egyptian dust plagued both man and beast. (Exodus 8:16-19)
➢ Flies came in swarms, bringing their contamination with them (which may have led to the next plague). (Exodus 8:20-32)

> Disease infected all the livestock, a catastrophe affecting business and their economies. (Exodus 9:1-7)
> Boils covered the bodies of both people and animals. (Exodus 9:8-12)
> Fire and hail decimated the region in the worst storm the nation had ever experienced. (Exodus 9:13-35)
> Locusts swarmed in, consuming all the vegetation not ravaged by the storm. (Exodus 10:1-20)
> Darkness that could be felt, for three days, halted all activity in the home, on the street, and throughout the land. (Exodus 10:21-29)
> Death of all the first-born throughout the land, from Pharaoh's palace, to the prisoner's cell, to the pasture. (Exodus 11:1 - 12:36)

There was another nation that came under God's judgment, though the outcome was much different. The story is found in the Old Testament in the few pages containing the story of a reluctant prophet named Jonah. God selected Jonah to carry a message of judgment and destruction to the nation of Nineveh. The elders of the land considered Jonah's message and led the nation in sorrowful repentance, changing God's mind on His judgment against them. God showed His great mercy and Nineveh was spared. (Read Jonah chapters 1-4)

Sometimes, judgment comes as a consequence of sinful acts. The righteousness of God includes holding leaders, citizens, and nations accountable for actions contrary to His standard of righteousness (*fairness and accuracy* in our lives, relationships, laws, courts, etc.).

This precept is critically important to those governing the free countries of the world. It is imperative that righteous citizens build upon the same foundation God provided. Paul described the accountability for such to the Corinthian church:

"Each one's work will become manifest, for the day will disclose it, because it will be revealed by fire, and the fire will test what sort of work each has done. If the work that anyone has built on the foundation survives, he will receive a reward." (1 Corinthians 3:14, ESV)

Exposure to this precept should lead each citizen to kneel in petition for ourselves, our leaders, and our country. We need God to send His Spirit drawing worshipers to His Kingdom who will infect the world with truth and righteousness – that His Kingdom would come to earth as it is in heaven, so people would live lives accountable to both God and their fellow man.

"...and (if) my people

who are called by my name

humble themselves and pray

and seek my face and

turn from their wicked ways,

then I will hear from heaven,

will forgive their sin

and will heal their land."

2 Chronicles 7:14

UNDERSTANDABLE 5 WORDS

"He will judge the world..."

Psalm 96:13

The most sobering thought in all of scripture is that God will judge everyone. No-one will be exempt from His righteous inspection. Evidence of such exists throughout the sacred texts. As we have already seen, He judges nations, and even acts in judgment toward both righteous and unrighteous acts in 'real-time' on earth. Examples of this are found in the lives of Adam and Eve, Moses, the reigns of Israel's and Judah's kings, Ananias and Saphira, Paul, etc. In fact, the breadth of biblical literature concerning God's judgments would be a book all in itself.

There is not a deed or a thought, not a word or any action that will evade the scrutiny of the Righteous One. The Bible reveals three things common to all: life, sin, and judgment after death.

The writer of Hebrews stated, *"...it is appointed for men to die once, and after this comes judgment."* (Hebrews 9:27)

In his letter to the Roman church, Paul made it clear that no-one could escape it:

"...do you suppose... you will escape the judgment of God? Or do you think lightly of the riches of His kindness and tolerance and patience, not knowing that the kindness of God leads you to repentance? But because of your stubbornness and unrepentant heart you are storing up wrath for yourself in the day of wrath and revelation of the righteous judgment of God." (Romans 2:3-5)

Paul later summarized the same precept to the Romans: *"So then each one of us will give an account of himself to God."* (Romans 14:12)

To the Corinthian church, Paul described it this way:

"For we must all appear before the judgment seat of Christ, so that each one may receive what is due for what he has done in the body, whether good or evil." (2 Corinthians 5:10)

Jesus told of the judgment awaiting us for every word spoken:

"...I tell you that every careless word that people speak, they shall give an accounting for it in the day of judgment. For by your words you will be justified, and by your words you will be condemned." (Matthew 12:36-37)

Many people develop an incorrect understanding of God's judgment from these words, thinking there is an eternal scale that weighs one's good deeds against one's bad deeds. The Bible tells us we are all sinners, and have all come short of God's glory. (Romans 3:23) Sin is simply rebellion against God's way; it is asserting our way over God's way. When we replace God's authority with our own hubris, we are – in essence – worshipping ourselves and our own ability to make the judgments for our lives. Paul's description to the Athenians reads: *"...He commands all people everywhere to repent, because He has fixed a day on which He will judge the world in righteousness..."* (Acts 17:30-31)

God desires that all agree with Him concerning the issue of sin. Sin separates us from God, but He made a provision for it through His Son, Jesus. It was Jesus' death on a cross that paid the penalty for our sin. He took the punishment for our offence to God. (Read Isaiah 53:1-12) The words that will justify us before God are simple; so simple a child can understand them. In fact, you can be justified by your faith in Jesus' sacrificial work on the cross – the payment for your sins, when you, with a sincere heart, utter a prayer similar to the one below:

Father God, I understand that
I am a sinner and that I have offended You.
I am sorry for this and I ask for Your forgiveness.
Thank You, Jesus, for dying on the cross
and taking the penalty of my sins.
I invite You to take over as the guide for my life.

These are the type of words Jesus said would justify us, for we cannot save ourselves; it is a work totally outside our ability to achieve. It is only by God's grace that we are enabled to be seen in His eyes as righteous (ready for heaven; ready to appear before the Holy and Righteous One). Jesus becomes our righteousness (Read 2 Corinthians 5:21).

After we have prayed the above prayer, whenever God looks at us, He sees Christ in us. It is Jesus that makes us fit to appear before the throne of judgment described in Revelation. (Read Revelation 20:11-15)

Jesus summarized the Believer's reprieve as passing from death to life:

> *"Truly, truly, I say to you,*
> *he who hears My word,*
> *and believes Him Who sent Me,*
> *has eternal life,*
> *and does not come into judgment,*
> *but has passed out of death into life."*
> (John 5:24)

Only those with the sobriety of righteous thought understand the necessity of building upon the foundation of the master builders whose resolute faith still rings true today:

"I entreat you in the most earnest manner to believe in Jesus Christ, for there is no salvation in any other... if you are not reconciled to God through Jesus Christ, if you are not clothed with the spotless robe of His righteousness, you must forever perish..."

From the last will and testament of:
John Witherspoon
Signer of the Declaration of Independence

Let us pray that leaders with such faith will guide this nation in generations to come.

"Remember that it is in God you live and move and have your being, – that, in the language of David, He is about your bed and about your path and spieth out all your ways – that there is not a thought in your hearts, nor a word upon your tongues, but lo! He knoweth them altogether, and that He will one day call you to a strict account for all your conduct in this mortal life."

William Samuel Johnson

Member of the Continental Congress, signer of the Constitution, framer of the Bill of Rights, U.S. Senator, Judge, and President of Columbia College.

Source: E. Edwards Beardsley, *Life and Times of William Samuel Johnson* (Boston: Houghton, Mifflin and Company, 1886), pp. 141-145.

UNDERSTANDABLE 5 WORDS

Thomas Jefferson described himself as a true disciple of the doctrines of Jesus Christ (see quote on p. 13). His conviction to preserve liberty's founding precepts are reflected in his own words:

"God Who gave us life gave us liberty. Can the liberties of a nation be secure when we have removed a conviction that these liberties are the gift of God? Indeed, I tremble for my country when I reflect that God is just, that His justice cannot sleep forever."

Source: Jefferson, Thomas, third president of The United States; quote emblazoned in the rotunda of the Jefferson Memorial.

UNDERSTANDABLE 5 WORDS

"...such a time as this..."

Esther 4:14

Freedom's signature has been drawn on the hearts of men and women of faith for thousands of years. One need only to browse the annals of history to find wonderful examples of women who embodied the patriot spirit to live free. Throughout history, women have been the unsung heroes of liberty. Freedom's fabric was sewn by those who chose to act as free servants of God, even under the rule of tyranny.

Though a slave, the mother of Moses acted in opposition to Egyptian law by hiding him for three months, then placing him in a waterproof basket which was placed in the Nile River where the Egyptian princess heard his cry and claimed him as her own. This child grew up to lead the nation of Israel out of slavery. (Read Exodus 2)

Many years later, the nation of Israel was conquered by the Persian army and taken into captivity for seventy years. It was during this time that another Persian king, pressured by his advisors, had his wife removed as queen for insubordination. Seeking a replacement for the queen, the king decreed that a nation-wide search would be made and the candidate would be selected through a beauty pageant. Like a flower in full bloom, so the beauty of orphaned Esther was recognized and she was awarded the esteemed role as queen.

Though she was queen, she was still a citizen of a people in subjection and rule by the Persians, one of whom despised the Jews and plotted to annihilate all Jews in the empire. The scheme was revealed to Mordecai, Esther's uncle, who had adopted and raised her upon her parents' death. Mordecai worked as a scribe in the king's court, recording the edicts and pronouncements of the king. He had actually saved the king on an earlier occasion when he discovered another plot by two palace officials planning an assassination. Freedom fighters seek the good of even their enemies to bridge the gap of bitterness caused by war.

Since the threat of extinction was imminent, and the plot had to be revealed, Esther risked her new appointment by appearing before the king unannounced – an action that could have resulted in her death. Before she approached the king, Mordecai advised her that, if she remained silent on the issue, God would bring deliverance at another time and she and her relatives would perish.

He then asked her to look at the situation from a historical perspective: *"And who knows whether you have not attained royalty for **such a time as this?**"* (Esther 4:14, bold added for emphasis)

Esther answered her uncle with a request to ask all the Jews in Shushan to fast and pray for three days, and that she and her friends would do the same. (Read Esther 4) When she approached her husband, the king, he looked favorably upon her and she revealed the evil plot, saving the nation from annihilation. (The book of Esther is in the Old Testament just before the book of Job, and its ten chapters are quickly read as the story is so well told.)

American women have also developed a legacy that is preserved in the annals of history. From settling the new land to protecting freedom today, women have been at the forefront of liberty's battle.

Our first president's mother, Mary Ball Washington, was widowed at the age of thirty-five with five children to raise. George was the oldest and only eleven at the time of his father's death, so it can be certain that from such an impressionable age to young adulthood, he was fashioned by the strong-willed matriarch who instilled in George the principles of honor to God and country. (**Source:** Murrow, Pamela, *Journal of the American Revolution: Ten Amazing Women of the Revolutionary War;* October 25, 2013)

Rosa Parks acted as a free woman when she refused to give up her seat in that bus on December 1, 1955. Years later she received the Presidential Medal of Freedom; the Congressional gold Medal; and, upon her death, was the first woman honored to be lain in state at the U.S. Capitol Building. (**Source:** www.thehenryford.org)

Martha Custis Washington traveled to her husband every winter bringing supplies and comfort to Washington and his troops. She provided nursing duties and organized a sewing circle with other officer's wives to repair uniforms, tents, and sleeping gear; and also made time to lead the officers wives in Bible study. Her tireless efforts were described by one observer:

"I never in my life knew a woman so busy from early morning until late at night as was Lady Washington, providing comforts for the sick soldiers." (**Source**: Roberts, Cokie. <u>Founding Mothers</u>, New York: Harper Collins, 2004, p. 94.)

Women have served our country in other wars as well. During World War Two, American women joined the war effort in The American Red Cross, factories, farms, as well as the military. Americans can thank God for the sacrifice given by thousands of women who seized the day in acting dutifully for God, family, and country. In fact, there is an effort to erect a memorial to honor women patriots of American history.

"The race is not to the swift, nor the battle to the strong; but the God of Israel is He, that giveth strength and power unto His people. Trust in Him at all times, ye people, pour out your hearts before Him; God is a refuge for us. Charlestown is laid in ashes. The battle began upon our entrenchments upon Bunker's Hill, Saturday morning about three o'clock, and has not ceased yet, and it is now three o'clock Sabbath afternoon... It is expected they will come over the Neck tonight, and a dreadful battle must ensue. *Almighty God, cover the heads of our countrymen, and be a shield to our dear friends.*"

Abigail Adams

Wife to President John Adams, writing to her husband on events close to home during the American Revolution

Source: Abigail Adams, <u>*Letters of Mrs. Adams, the wife of John Adams*</u>. to John Adams on June 18, 1775.

Will you echo Mrs. Adams' prayer and let her faith resonate in your heart?

"…you are… one in Christ…"

Galatians 3:28

The United States of America is unique among nations in her origins and composition. It has long been known that the pilgrims came to the shores of Massachusetts in search of the opportunity to worship without the constraints of the national Church of England. The Native Americans assisted the early settlers through the harsh winter.

As our country grew people from many nations began arriving. During the gold rush of 1849 the world heard of America's streets being paved with gold. There were actually people who arrived here wanting to see the golden streets only to be bitterly disappointed... but many of those same people developed a tenacity to endure and persevere through hardship, making a life for themselves and the families they brought with them.

Immigrants from China, Germany, Scotland, Ireland, Wales, Italy, Greece, and other countries, as well as those who entered our land as slaves from various parts of Africa were all threads to a great fabric being woven by the hand of The Master Weaver. The freedom experiment is ever evolving toward broader diversity, a richer history, deeper generational roots in pursuit of happiness, and greater potential in impacting the world for good because of the blessings of the One Who is known by His goodness.

Luke, a physician who meticulously wrote the biography of Jesus, continued his work in writing what we know as the New Testament book of Acts. He describes an event that occurred as people were gathered in Jerusalem for the Passover (a Jewish holiday commemorating the great exodus). Jesus' disciples had just drawn lots to determine who would replace Judas, who committed suicide after betraying Jesus. Before this crucial decision, the group spent a significant amount of time in prayer. After the lot fell to Matthias, they continued to pray and wait on the One Jesus had promised would come to guide them in all truth. (Read Acts 1:1-8) Then, a rush of wind came through the place where they were meeting and what appeared as tiny tongues of fire appeared, resting over the head of each follower, followed by a cacophony of languages that erupted in the room, creating such an audible commotion that others who had arrived in Jerusalem followed the clamor to discover its cause.

Luke described the peculiar occurrence:

"Now, there were Jews living in Jerusalem, devout men from every nation under heaven. And when this sound occurred, the crowd came together, and was bewildered because each one of them was hearing them speak in his own language."

Luke continued the description, writing:

"... how is it that we each hear them in our own language...? Parthian and Medes and Elamites, and residents of Mesopotamia, Judea and Cappadocia, Pontus and Asia, Phrygia and Pamphylia, Egypt and the districts of Libya around Cyrene, and visitors from Rome, both Jews and proselytes, Cretans and Arabs – we hear them in our own tongues speaking of the mighty deeds of God." (Acts 2:5-12)

What an incredible scene this must have been – for all these ethnic groups to hear the same message of hope through Jesus Christ, the mighty work of God toward mankind! In a remarkable way, this is a picture of America's mission: to be a safe haven for all and to broadcast the origin of that freedom to all people groups.

Though many nations now have various ethnic groups within their borders, I postulate the probability that no nation is as diverse as the United States. If America can navigate through the complexities of amalgamating the diversity of nationalities among us, we will only make a stronger case for freedom's cause and enduring value. The 2015 Charleston community's response to a vicious hate crime that took the lives of nine people points to God's power for healing and restoration. This is all the more reason why Christians must accept the call of Christ to connect hearts to the heart of God.

Only the visible, real love of God will bridge the great disparity of customs in our towns and cities. Political correctness doesn't work. It does nothing more than create deeper fractures in a diverse society. Why? It does not come from the wellspring of truth. It is only a veneer, or at best a confederate, impersonating acceptance and tolerance which only makes bad matters worse.

We see the clash of cultures almost daily in our national news and many wonder if anything can be done to reconcile these people groups. Christians have the answer that can be announced across this nation and around the world… we are one in Christ. **We can pray for reconciliation and peace in this land and around the world. Let the prayer for reconciliation between cultures reverberate in your life as you seek to build bridges between people groups.**

"There is neither Jew nor Greek, there is neither slave nor free man, there is neither male nor female; for you are all one in Christ Jesus."
Galatians 3:28

UNDERSTANDABLE **5** WORDS

"I have written to you..."

I John 2:14

The disciple whom Jesus loved was writing to encourage the first century church to continue in pursuit of happiness by exercising God's love to all and to follow the precepts of God's Word as Jesus had instructed. In fact, he stated from the beginning of the letter that he was only expressing the very things his fellow disciples and he had seen and heard from their time with Jesus, and the joy of articulating his thoughts was completed by telling others!

So, I take this moment to say that the discovery and development of this book was an extraordinary joy to experience. However, sharing it with you completes my joy in knowing that more people might: search God's Word through the inspiration of *five understandable words*; apply it to their lives; and share its light to others who walk in a world darkened by the curse of sin.

Early in the book of Deuteronomy, Moses records God's words describing the choice the young nation had before them. It was a choice between a blessing or a curse. He prepares their hearts by describing God's rich provision to those who follow the precepts in His Word:

> ➤ He would give them great cities.
> ➤ He would fill their homes with good things.
> ➤ He would supply plenty of food and water.
> (**Source:** Deuteronomy 6:10-11)

Moses then continues to record God's directives:

> *"You should diligently keep the commandments of the Lord your God,*
> *and His testimonies and His statutes*
> *which He has commanded you.*
> *You shall do what is right and good in the sight of the Lord,*
> *that it may be well with you."*
> (Deuteronomy 6:17-18)

Several chapters later, God provides yet more benefits to trusting His way:

➤ The tenure of their government would be extended.
(Deuteronomy 11:9)
➤ There would be plenty of milk and honey to consume and trade. (Deuteronomy 11:9)
➤ There would be plenty of rain for their crops, grapes, and olive trees. (Deuteronomy 11:14)
➤ Their cattle would be supplied with plenty of grass for feeding.
(Deuteronomy 11:15)
➤ There will be plenty for their families to be nourished and satisfied. (Deuteronomy 11:15)

God then sets before them the choice:

- **The Blessing:** possessing the land and enjoying the life of liberty and plenty that God promised.
  + the blessing will extend in the country and in the cities.
  + the blessing will be applied to the children, as well as to the offspring of their herds.
  + even their baskets and kneading bowls would show God's blessings.
  + the blessing will follow them going out as well as coming back in.
  + the blessing will give them victory in battle.
  + the blessing will be evidenced through the work of their hands.
  + the blessing will enable the nation to lend to other nations while being a debtor to none.
  + the blessing will position the nation above all other nations.

- **The Curse:** *losing* all the blessings of God's favor in the country or city:
  - loss of their homes and land.
  - loss of their livelihood.
  - loss of health for child-bearing.
  - loss of the protection in battle.
  - loss of financial power to lend, and
  - becoming burdened by debt.

And that was just the tip of the iceberg curse. (**Source:** Deuteronomy 28:1-68)

The Founders of our country were intimately familiar with the ancient biblical texts and sought to convey such in their speeches, their sermons (over 80% were ministers), and in the development of the founding documents (*The Articles of Confederation, The Declaration of Independence, The Constitution,* and *The Bill of Rights*). Our nation is vitally tied to her source of liberty, and to reject such spells certain doom for this great nation.

It seems painfully obvious that history has marked the *blessings* this country enjoyed from its birth, as well as the evidence of the *curse* when the nation departed from righteousness (remember the discussion on *fairness and accuracy*?). Once a nation strays from the principles of righteousness, the obvious signs of the curse raise their ugly heads: the weather patterns ruin crops, destroying the source of food for man and cattle alike; debt erodes prosperity; corruption increases; freedoms decrease; and the houses of worship become empty.

Turn back from pride; turn away from self centered ways; seek God's face; intercede for our country and ask God to heal our land. Pray like it all depends on you, while trusting God with the outcome.

UNDERSTANDABLE 5 WORDS

Elias Boudinot
on
The Bible

"For nearly half a century have I anxiously and critically studied that invaluable treasure; and I still scarcely ever take it up that I do not find something new – that I do not receive some valuable addition to my stock of knowledge or perceive some instructive fact never observed before. In short, were you to ask me to recommend the most valuable book in the world, I should fix on the Bible as the most instructive both to the wise and ignorant. Were you to ask me for one affording the most rational and pleasing entertainment to the inquiring mind, I should repeat, it is the Bible; and should you renew the inquiry for the best philosophy or the most interesting history, I should still urge you to look into your Bible. I would make it, in short, the Alpha and Omega of knowledge."

PRESIDENT OF CONGRESS; SIGNED THE PEACE TREATY TO END THE AMERICAN REVOLUTION; FIRST ATTORNEY ADMITTED TO THE U. S. SUPREME COURT BAR; FRAMER OF THE BILL OF RIGHTS; DIRECTOR OF THE U. S. MINT

(**Source:** Elias Boudinot, The Age of Revelation, or the Age of Reason Shewn to be An Age of Infidelity (Philadelphia: Asbury Dickins, 1801))

Epilogue

We have taken a journey through the sacred texts of The Bible to discover precepts that provided our founding fathers a foundation that could be used in forming the documents so many now take for granted. The liberties we know are not guaranteed; they come at the cost of continued vigilance for the protection and proliferation of our worldview both domestically and internationally.

It is impossible for mankind to ignore the declaration of righteousness by the grandeur of creation, and we have seen how the Founders warned future generations of disregarding the Light of the world and the devastating consequences of ignoring those warnings. Those who would act in such a way only prove their determination to remain fools for failure, repeating history's mistakes, with no backbone to stand for what is right and good.

God's Word was breathed into the hearts and minds of those who surrendered to His way. This same Word spoke everything into existence and became flesh, dwelling among mankind. The wisdom this Word provides leads to the rescue of a single soul, a family, a community, a region, a nation, and a fallen world.

Freedom is not certain for the next generation. Every responsible, moral citizen must take hold of the baton of God's Word and teach its precepts to those who follow. It cannot be done casually; it must be an intentional, diligent effort to instruct the next generation to seek out the path of God's Kingdom, that it might be the pattern for a world order of true peace.

Knowing Whose we are makes it crystal clear the path we are to take in service to our country. Through service to the Creator we guarantee the success of our efforts at developing national communities that offer peace and freedom. Every nation that embraces this approach will shine with the greatness of God's righteousness, attracting other nations to its light. These precepts can be exported through those who arrive on our shores and who will carry the absolutes of independence around the world.

As we conform to the guidance of God's law we are personally transformed. Leaving the walk of darkness, we can then be agents God uses to transform our nation and world; opening into an era of light and life. It doesn't come easy and requires great perseverance. One example of God's transforming power is seen in freedom's continued development through, *"the emancipation of slavish parts of mankind all over the earth."* (**Source:** from the notes of John Adams development of, *"A Dissertation on the Canon and Feudal Law"*, February, 1765)

Any enslaved people hope to live free. Though slavery's wicked head was not severed until the Civil War, many of the Founders opposed slavery and the duplicity of those who would support the Declaration of Independence while still enabling an economic system that enabled the enslavement of people. John Adams and his son, John Quincy Adams both opposed slavery. It was John Quincy Adams that exclaimed, *"Blessed, forever blessed, be the name of God,"* after succeeding in rescinding the Gag Rule that had prohibited the discussion of slavery in Congress. (**Source:** Diary entry of December 3, 1844) Years before, Richard Bassett, a signer of the Constitution, converted to Christianity during the Revolutionary War, freeing his slaves and then hiring those who would work for him in wages. In fact, even before The Revolution, there were Methodist African-Americans that preached strongly against slavery within the Methodist tradition along the Yadkin River Valley. (**Source:** August 13, 1587. Roanoke Settlement-The Lost Colony. The world Book Encyclopedia, Vol. 12, p. 5732.)

Patrick Henry was so moved by Anthony Benezet's book against the slave trade that he wrote of his empowered conviction against slavery:

"It is not amazing, that at a time when the rights of humanity are defined... with precision... we find men... adopting a principle as repugnant to humanity, as it is inconsistent to the Bible? ... I will not, I cannot justify it... I believe a time will come when an opportunity will be offered to abolish this lamentable evil... It is a debt we owe to the purity of our Religion to show that it is a variance with that law which warrants slavery... A serious review... gives gloomy perspective to future times." (**Source:** Federer, William J., "America's God and Country, Enclyclopedia of Quotations, 2013; p. 288.)

The well of fortitude is fed by the spring of hope we carry to the world. This hope is certain and is of an eternal Kingdom that will never end. It will take those with great fortitude to stand firm, seek peace, and pursue it. We must be willing to take the mantle of responsibility for preparing, equipping, and bequeathing our inalienable rights to the next generation. The example of: our confident hope in God's precepts; our courage nourished by the confidence we place in God; and our commitment to seek unity in diversity through the love of liberty's Author, will ensure the tranquility and stability of our nation for those who will take our place. Martin Luther King spoke eloquently on the matter:

"I have a dream that one day... the sons of former slaves and the sons of former slave-owners will be able to sit down together at the table of brotherhood... that my four little children will one day live in a nation where they will not be judged by the color of their skin, but by the content of their character." (**Source:** Ibid, p. 353)

The Bible instructs us to look to the ancient paths, the good way, and walk in them to find peace in living. (Jeremiah 6:16). Notice that the writer instructs the reader to take the ancient path that is the good way. There are surely ancient paths that lead to destruction – a bad way. Those who ignore God's way are bound to repeat the failures of history. Our forefathers and foremothers sought out the ancient paths and discerned the way that led to a good future. They were women and men of great confidence in the precepts established by a righteous God. We admire the fortitude they displayed in establishing this great nation. Shouldn't we also follow their guidance by walking in those same paths of righteousness to secure our country's future?

So, I leave you with these *five understandable words*:

"*Proclaim liberty throughout the land...*"
(Leviticus 25:10)

sf

Five Understandable Words ©
Source
IN ALPHABETICAL ORDER

Biblical Passages Quoted
In Biblical Order

Biblical Passages Referenced
In Order of Appearance

Historical Works Cited
In Order of Appearance

1. Lincoln, Abraham; <u>Complete Works of Abraham Lincoln</u>, John G. Nicolay and John Hay, editors (New York: Tandy-Thomas Company, 1894), Vol. VIII, pp. 235-236, Proclamation Appointing a National Fast Day, March 30, 1863. (p. viii)
2. *The Works of Alexander Hamilton*, John Church Hamilton, editor (New York: John F. Trow, 1850), Vol. II, p. 80, "The Farmer Refuted." (p. xv)
3. Leviticus 25:10 emblazoned on the Liberty Bell; 110th Congress, 1st Session, H. RES. 888, December 8, 2007. (p. 3)
4. Jay, William, *The Life of John Jay: With Selections From His Correspondence and Miscellaneous Papers* (New York: J. and J. Harper, 1833), Vol. I, pp. 457-458, to the Committee of the Corporation of the City of New York on June 29, 1826. (p. 10)
5. Randall, Henry S., *The Life of Thomas* Jefferson (NY: Derby and Jackson, 1958), Vol. 3, p. 451, Letter to Charles Thompson, January 9, 1816. (p. 13)
6. Rankin, J.E., Sermon Preached in the First Congregational Church, Washington, D.C., January 16th, 1876. (p. 14)
7. The Mayflower Compact; paragraph 2, line 2; 1620. (p. 17)
8. www.pilgrimhallmuseum.org,(p. 17)
9. *Journal of the House of the Representatives of the United States of America* (Washington, DC: Cornelius Wendell, 1855), 34th Cong., 1st Sess., p. 354, January 23, 1856. (p. 18)
10. Richmond v. Moore, 107 Ill. 429, 1883 WL 10319 (Ill.), 47 Am. Rep. 445 (Ill. 1883). (p. 21)
11. Penn, William, Fundamental Constitutions of Pennsylvania, 1682.) (p. 26)
12. Story, Joseph, *Life and Letters of Joseph Story*, William W. Story, ed. (Boston: Charles C. Little and James Brown, 1851), Vol. II, p. 8. (p. 29)
13. Henry, Patrick, *Patrick Henry: Life, Correspondence and Speeches*, William Wirt Henry, ed. (New York: Charles Scribner's Sons, 1891), Vol. II, p. 592, to Archibald Blair on January 8, 1799. (p. 38)
14. The Debates and Proceedings in the Congress of the United States, Joseph Gales, ed. (Washington: Gales and Seaton, 1834), Vol. I, p. 27) (p.42)
15. Franklin, Benjamin, *The Writings of Benjamin Franklin*, Jared Sparks, ed. (Boston: Tappan, Whittemore and Mason, 1840), Vol. X, p. 297, April 17, 1787.) (p. 45)
16. Webster, Daniel, *The Works of Daniel Webster,* 1851, Vol. I. (p. 46)
17. Adams, Samuel, The Writings of Samuel Adams, Henry Alonzon Cushing, ed. (New York: G. P. Putnam's Sons, 1908), Vol. IV, p. 356, "to the Legislature of Massachusetts, January 17, 1794. (p. 49)
18. Choules, John Overton August 12, 1843, in the Preface to the 1844 reprint of Daniel Neal's, "History of the Puritans", 1731. (p. 54)
19. Adams, John, *The Works of John Adams, Second President of the United States*, Charles Francis Adams, ed. (Boston: Charles C. Little and James Brown, 1851), Vol. VI, p. 9. (p. 60)

20. Webster, Noah, *The Holy Bible in the Common Version with Amendments of the Language;* 1833. (p. 63)

21. Rush, Benjamin, *Essays, Literary, Moral and Philosophical* (Philadelphia: Thomas and Samuel F. Bradford, 1798), pp. 94, 100, "A Defence of the Use of the Bible as a School Book." (p. 64)

22. Rush, Benjamin, *Essays, Literary, Moral & Philosphical* (Philadelphia: Thomas & Samuel F. Bradford, 1798), p. 112, "A Defense of the Use of the Bible as a School Book." (p. 68)

23. *Heart Throbs,* Volume Two [ed. Joseph Mitchell Chappell] (Boston: Chappel Pub. Co., 1911), pp. ii, 1-2. (p. 70)

24. Boudinot, Elias, *The Life, Public Services, Addresses, and Letters of Elias Boudinot,* J. J. Boudinot, ed. (Boston: Houghton, Mifflin and Co., 1896), Vol. I, pp. 19, 21, speech in the First Provincial Congress of New Jersey. (p. 75)

25. Adams, John, *Works,* Vol. II, pp. 6-7, diary entry for February 22, 1756. (p. 80)

26. Bush, George, *Heartbeat: George Bush in His Own Words* [Citadel Press-Kensington Pub. Corp., NY]: p. 149. (p. 84)

27. Kennedy, Robert F., www.RFKcenter.org. Speech in Capetown, South Africa, June 6, 1966. (p. 87)

28. *Life of John Quincy Adams,* W. H. Seward, ed. (Auburn, NY: Derby, Miller and Company, 1849), p. 248. (p. 88)

29. President Lyndon B. Johnson, State of the Union address before Congress, January 5, 1965. (p. 90)

30. Adoption of the national motto; P.L. 84-140, US Government Publishing Office; www.gpo.gov (p. 91)

31. Roosevelt, Theodore, "Our Nation, A Product of Christianity," *Springfield Republican,* 1884, editorial. (p. 96)

32. *Letters of Delegates to Congress: January 1, 1776-May 15, 1776,* Paul H. Smith, editor (Washington DC: Library of Congress, 1978), Vol. 3, pp. 502-503, Oliver Wolcott to Laura Wolcott on April 10, 1776. (p. 103)

33. Proclamation reprinted in the Columbian Centinal, April 4, 1798. (p. 106)

34. *Declaration of Independence,* paragraph 2. (p. 110)

35. Lazarus, Emma, 1849-1887, Read at the opening Ceremonies for the Statue of Liberty. (p. 118)

36. Paine, Thomas, Common Sense. 3rd edition, 1776. (p. 122)

37. Adams, John Quincy, *The Jubilee of the Constitution* (New York: Samuel Colman, 1839), (p. 123)

38. Aristedes Apology (Report) to Emporer Hadrian; Kirby, Peter. "Historical Jesus Theories." *Early Christian Writings.* 2015) (p. 124)

39. Clarkson, Thomas, *Memoirs of the Private and Public Life of William Penn* (London: Longman, Hunt, Rees, Orme, and Brown, 1813), Vol. I, p. 303. (p. 132)

40. Willard, Samuel, 1640-1707, Quoting from the Library of American Literature by Stedman and Hutchinson, 1889. *The Christian History of the Constitution of the United States of* America, Compiled by Verna M. Hall, Edited by Joseph Allan Montgomery [The Iversen Associates Press, NY], p. 396. (p. 132)

41. 1796 Washington's Farewell Address. (p. 135)

42. Rush, Benjamin, *Letters of Benjamin Rush*, L. H. Butterfield, ed. (Princeton, NJ: Princeton University Press, 1951), Vol. II, p. 936, to John Adams, January 23, 1807. (p. 136)

43. The Massachusetts Centinal, Wednesday, August 15, 1787. (p. 140)

44. The last will and testament, John Witherspoon, Signer of the Declaration of Independence. (p. 148)

45. Beardsley, E. Edwards, *Life and Times of William Samuel Johnson* (Boston: Houghton, Mifflin and Company, 1886), pp. 141-145. (p. 150)

46. Jefferson, Thomas, third president of The United States; quote emblazoned in the rotunda of the Jefferson Memorial. (p. 152)

47. Murrow, Pamela, Journal of the American Revolution, *Ten Amazing Women of the Revolutionary War;* October 25, 2013. (p. 155)

48. Roberts, Cokie, Founding Mothers, New York: Harper Collins, 2004, 94. (p. 156)

49. Adams, Abigail, *Letters of Mrs. Adams, the wife of John Adams*. *With an Introductory Memoir by Her Grandson, Charles Francis Adams*. (Boston: Charles C. Little and James Brown, 1840), p. 40, to John Adams on June 18, 1775). (p. 156)

50. Boudinot, Elias, *The Age of Revelation, or the Age of Reason Shewn to be An Age of Infidelity* (Philadelphia: Asbury Dickins, 1801). (p. 166)

51. Adams, John, from the notes of John Adams' development of, *"A Dissertation of the Canon and Feudal Law"*, February, 1765; America's God and Country – Encylopedia of Quotations, compiled by William J. Federer, p. 5. (p. 168)

52. Adams, John Quincy, personal entry in his diary, Deceember 3, 1844; Ibid, p. 20. (p. 168)

53. Ibid, p. 39. (p. 168)

54. Henry, Patrick, personal letter to Robert Pleasants, January 18, 1773; Ibid, p. 288. (p. 168-169)

55. King, Martin Luther, from the speech, *"I Have a Dream"*, presented on August 28, 1963 at the National March for Civil Rights; Ibid, p. 353. (p. 169)

56. *The Collected Works of Abraham Lincoln,* Roy P. Basler, ed., Volume VI, "Proclamation of Thanksgiving" (October 3, 1863), p. 497. (p. 182)

Founding documents such as *The Declaration of Independence* are cited with great appreciation to the founding fathers and the National Archives, Washington, DC.

Bloom, B.S., Engelhart, M.D., Furst, E.J., Hill, W.H., Krathwuhl, D.R., *Taxonomy of Educational Objectives: The Classification of Eductional Goals* (NY: David McKay, Co.), 1956. (p. 66)

Also see: www.womensmemorial.org per page 156.

Written Prose Cited
In Alphabetical Order

1. *America*, by Samuel Francis Smith, 1831. (pp. 8, 53)
2. *America, the Beautiful*, by Katherine Lee Bates, 1893. (pp. 49, 71, 127)
3. *Battle Hymn of the Republic*, by Julia Ward Howe, 1861 (p. 36-37)
4. *How Firm a Foundation*, attributed to George Keith, 1787 (p. 106)
5. *The New Colossus*, by Emma Lazarus, 1883. (p. 118)
6. *The Star Spangled Banner*, by Francis Scott Key, 1814 (pp. 33, 91)
7. *Success*, by Bessie Anderson Stanley, *Heart Throbs, Volume Two* [ed. Joseph Mitchell Chappell] (Boston: Chappel Pub. Co., 1911), pp. ii, 1-2. (p. 70) [Note: In the publication, the work was actually attributed to anonymous.]

"I... fervently implore the inter-position of the Almighty Hand to heal the wounds of the nation and to restore it as soon as may be consistent with the Divine purposes to the full enjoyment of peace, harmony, tranquility and union."

Abraham Lincoln

Source: *The Collected Works of Abraham Lincoln,* Roy P. Basler, ed., Volume VI, "Proclamation of Thanksgiving" (October 3, 1863), p. 497.

"Blessed is the nation whose God is the Lord."

Psalm 33:12